FREEDOM FROM

THE WEB OF KARMA

Through

Rising Energy Practice

Acharya Premananda

ACKNOWLEDGMENTS

A special thank you goes to my wife and partner Shambhavi Devi. She has contributed greatly to the book with ideas concerning what to take out and what to add. She has also done excellent editing work in the formulation of the topics presented. She is herself a very serious practitioner of Rising Energy Practice and she knows, through personal experience, the challenges and rewards of deep practice and transformation. I am grateful to her for her patient participation in getting the edited manuscript ready for publication. Perhaps most importantly, I appreciate that my life with her contributes greatly to keeping me humble and honest.

I am very grateful for the profound transformation set in motion through contact with my spiritual teacher Swami Rudrananda (called Rudi in the following).1 I am also grateful to other teachers, fellow practitioners, and students who have in various ways contributed to my inner development.

CONTENTS

PREFACE

This book was first published in Norwegian by Rudrananda Press, Oslo, Norway in 2006. The first English edition was published in 2011 under my then author name Swami Ganeshananda. The present edition represents an effort to update, revise and expand the book based on circumstances and insights that have occurred in the years since publishing the first edition. I have taken out some material from the first edition and have added new sections throughout the book. I have made changes in places where I felt it would add to and complement the overall quality. It is my sincere hope that this edition will be of help to people interested in meditation practice and inner growth.

To Creative Energy

She's in us and we are Her;
She's all that can occur.
She's in all that was before
and in all that will appear,
She's in all that we are seeing
and in everything we hear.
She's the ocean and the waves,
the stillness and the flow;
She's the veil and the Grace,
the shadows and the glow.

I bow down to Her;
She is the source
of all I ever was
and all that I may be.
She rises from my base
as purifying energy,
unfolding Her Grace,
piercing the centers
before She enters
the crown of infinity
in an ultimate embrace.

I am Her and She is me!

1

RISING ENERGY

There are many ways and levels of practicing meditation. If we want to transform ourselves from being stuck in and limited by the tensions and patterns of ego identity into an awareness of deeper essence, then it is necessary to find a practice that can help bring about that transformation. It is also important to commit to a long-term process using the chosen practice.

I have practiced and built upon what I learned from my teacher Rudi in the years since he passed away in the early seventies. I call it *Rising Energy Practice*. This name refers to the fact that we transcend the problems and limitations of our individual self by merging into a higher awareness of the universal Self. It also refers to the fact that the practice makes the energy rise in the spine to purify the psychic system.

Rising Energy Practice is a very powerful way to transform tensions and attachments into energy flow and universal awareness. The process I have gone through over the years has shown me that it is a very effective practice, provided there is a deep commitment to it and that it is used regularly, no matter what the outer circumstances of life.

Melting Inner Ice

The vast majority of people in modern society is more or less stressed and limited by tensions and mental/emotional blocks. Such tensions and blocks represent life force (energy) under pressure. I call tensions *crystallizations of energy*, frozen over time through the development of a limited ego and identity. Tensions and blocks are like layers of ice in the psychic system, keeping the life force from flowing unhindered. In so doing, it causes physical, mental and emotional suffering. This crystallization is the cause of what I call *the web of karma*.

Fortunately, the very common suffering of being caught in this web can be dissolved through conscious inner work. It can be transformed from something that catches us into something that shines in and on us as the unobstructed light of consciousness. Another way of saying it is that the psychic ice that constitutes the web of karma can be melted by regularly and deeply bringing the heat of meditative attention to the crystallization within us. The Rising Energy Practice is one way of accomplishing that.

A central tool in the Rising Energy Practice is the double breathing exercise. It is really quite a simple inner exercise, but it takes diligent exploration over time to discover what it can do. It can go very deep and it can be extremely effective. Going into the heart with the breath and attention, and then into the chakras below, these energy centers open more and more. It is quite endless. In that opening, we begin to recognize the Oneness and the powerful life force at the core of being. What was a set of problems before now becomes an open limitless space with subtle and powerful energy flowing in it. This can be recognized more and more as we practice regularly.

The main purpose of the Rising Energy Practice is to keep attention deeply within the psychic system, beyond the analytical and judging mind. Keeping the attention on the breath and chakras, we ask deeply for the whole psychic system to open. Through practice, frozen tensions, patterns and blocks melt in the system and flow down to the base of the spine. In the process this flow heats up through inner attention until it becomes a kind of steam that spontaneously rises up the spine to the top of the head. This is the Kundalini, the basic creative energy of life.

As this fine and powerful creative force awakens in awareness and ascends, our chakra system is cleansed and strengthened; it is made more open and balanced. Psychic scars and residues (samscaras) developed throughout life are dissolved by the rising energy.

When the energy reaches the thousand pedaled lotus chakra at the crown of the head, increased wisdom and compassion is created. Recognition of the essential Oneness at the core of life is accomplished as the individual life force at the base of the spine merges with its universal source coming in at the top of the head. As we open to this source and allow it to fill us, the universal dimension gradually becomes the dominant vibration in our awareness and expression.

This transformation process can be quite strong at times, particularly if we have tensions and patterns that are very deep and have been frozen for a long time. However, it can also be a much softer process. Both have their built in challenges. Whichever way it manifests, it is important not to succumb to fear and doubt as tensions and patterns dissolve.

In the case of a strong transformation process, we have to go through a stage which can be quite uncomfortable in that it may feel like we are in the middle of a tunnel that we do not see the end of. We may feel trapped and tempted to give up because the transformation is so strong that it requires a lot of energy, making us feel drained. It may seem overwhelmingly difficult to move on. At this stage, it is important to keep the attention inside on the practice so that we can move forward steadily step by step into the light at the end of the tunnel. Here, a whole new landscape of possibilities and realizations is waiting to show itself.

In the case of a soft and slow transformation process, there is a danger of losing sight of the fact that things are actually going on within the psychic system. It can be very subtle and hard to notice on day to day bases. In this case, it can be tempting to just give up because not much seems to be happening.

To help us feel secure and inspired in the transformation process, whichever form it takes, having regular support and nourishment is very helpful. To that end, it is good to work with a teacher we trust and who is capable of giving us the needed nourishment in the form of energy. For additional support and challenge, it is also good to practice in a group.

Through the Eyes

A most important aspect of Rising Energy Practice is Open Eyes Meditation with a teacher. The energy exchange that occurs in this type of meditation is very uplifting and nourishing, though it can be challenging to work through natural resistance, tension and blocks that usually stand in the way of the transformative process it invites. Staying centered in the heart and the whole energy system within while not being lost in the head is the big challenge that so easily becomes apparent when working this way.

In this form of meditation the teacher's job is to be immersed in the Self, the universal core of being. In a state of centeredness, energy flow, awareness and compassion, the teacher transmits a deeply nourishing energy to practitioners. During Open Eyes Meditation, practitioners sit and work inside while tuning in to the deeper Self, using the teacher as a contact point and doorway into awareness of that Self. A profound heart to heart contact can be established. This can have a subtle but profound impact on each practitioner's state of being. The more a practitioner opens to the contact, the more the impact is intensified.

The practitioner's heart and awareness can open wide through the contact, first in glimpses, then for longer periods, and finally as a state the person is capable of entering at will. The dualism of teacher and student can gradually dissolve and become an experience of energy flow and Oneness. Recognition of the basic life force can be awakened. The process can melt inner crystallization. Existential anxiety can become inner work and expanded energy flow. Liberation can happen. Through practice, the deeper Self can be glimpsed and eventually fully recognized.

Open Eyes Meditation is a form of *shaktipat*, which literally means *descent of grace*. It can be received through a teacher in four different ways: *Look, touch, thought or speech*. In the Tantric tradition, shaktipat invites the initiated person into the deepest aspect of a human being: the fundamental creative energy and awareness. Shaktipat can ignite a flame in the practitioner and support the unfolding of an inner liberation process. It can set in motion a process that makes it possible to recognize and live from the unconditional love hidden in the heart.

At the start of this practice, and at various times along the transformation process, people can experience a band of tension around the head, and/or tightness around the heart as well as in the lower chakras. These are tangible effects of being caught in the web of karma. I certainly had a lot of that when I started, and also at various stages along the way since then. It can be an uncomfortable transformation to work through, but in time, with regular practice, the chakras open up. The third eye chakra opens, the heart opens much more than before, and gradually more energy flow can be felt in the lower chakras as a result of inner asking and letting go. These are the rewards of working through discomforts along the way.

Throughout the growth process it is very important to be grounded in a solid feeling of connection with the earth and with the life that we have at this moment. We need to be grounded in the here and now as a base for going into the infinite. The elements of the life we have at the moment of practice should be consciously related to as a source of nourishment and not as a set of constricting problems.

As we work inside, the chakras open up more and more, allowing for a different perspective and life experience. The inner work opens us to many new experiences and possibilities. There is more flow in the chakra system and more joy and gratitude in the heart. Contact with the deeper Self attracts a more expanded range of options in everyday life and a more profound experience of joy and energy in everything attracted.

Working Our Way Back

Texts that explain the process of growth resulting from tantric practices say that at the core of human beings and all manifestation there is *dynamic stillness*, a space of unlimited potential in which fundamental creative energy vibrates. The stillness is not dead; it is full of potential. It is silence with the fundamental force of creation vibrating in it. This extremely fine and powerful energy unfolds as everything in the universe. Within the stillness everything emerges. Dynamic stillness is the source of all emerging manifestation and of all life. It is the source of *our* life. As such, it is our deepest Self.

Dynamic stillness describes both the *Shiva* and *Shakti* aspects of fundamental reality. Shiva is the stillness of unlimited potential. *Shakti (Kundalini on the human level)* is the dynamic aspect, the energy unfolding within the silent potential. Anything can happen in this dynamic stillness, anytime, anywhere. It is the source of all being and manifestation. Shakti vibrates in the unlimited potential of Shiva and emerges as all manifestation. Shakti becomes whatever is natural for it to become. This infinite reality at the core of being can be recognized by bringing our attention deeper than our ego identity. We recognize it by opening ourselves to the inexplicable mystery of existence. Through Rising Energy Practice we work our way back to the source of our being, to the dynamic stillness we have come from and are ever emerging from. This is a process that can be thought of as emergence in reverse. We work our way backwards through our tensions and layers of physical, mental and emotional manifestation to the essence from which we have emerged and are continuously emerging. This is a liberation from ego self by merging into the deeper Self.

Intention

When we sit down to practice, it is important to feel our body first, to be alert and relaxed, and to be focused on the wish to grow. Being aware of our intention is a powerful tool. Why are we sitting in meditation? Why are we turning our attention inside? We may hear our inner voice respond clearly with something like: *"I'm sitting down because I want to open up and grow. I want to feel my deeper universal nature. I don't want to be stuck in this problem-focused limited identity"*. Or, simply, *"I wish to grow."* Clear intention expressed in attention turned inward with a deep wish in the heart makes the practice quite powerful.

We can feel the power of our wish and willingness to open and let go. We may notice that when we are stressed, distracted and unfocused, things become a lot more challenging. The more we worry, analyze and think, the bigger whatever we are struggling with tends to get. On the other hand, when we get quiet and focused inwardly, spontaneous transformation tends to happen. Creativity begins to arise very naturally from the depth within us. Useful ideas and actions begin to unfold. It is very simple, but the process requires a great deal of inner attention, patience and perseverance.

As we work inside, it is usual to feel some resistance, agitation and tension. We may feel doubt and confusion. This is mental noise that we can gradually dissolve by systematically placing the attention on the breath and chakras, and by opening and letting go into our inner center of being. Through this simple practice, an awareness of pure *I am* begins to emerge. It may take a lot of time and inner attention, but eventually it may dawn on us that we are not the problems, emotions and thoughts we have been so preoccupied with due to our conditioning. We are not really limited by our ego identity, pain, doubt or fear. Instead, we are simply an expression of that deeper stillness which has creative energy vibrating in it, all the time, everywhere. It dawns on us that there is Oneness, and that we and everything are it. We have just not recognized it before because of the mental and emotional noise obstructing it.

Even after having done this practice every day now for almost fifty years, it is still not boring. It is fresh. Life continuously brings new challenges, and it can be discovered again and again that *"oh, that too is just energy under pressure".* It is simply the web of karma which essentially is a web of tension and attachment. Once we let go of that tension and attachment, the web becomes a source of transcendence and freedom. We rise by that which we fell before. We see that all the layers of our identity are just emerging from the source of being. We recognize more and more deeply that we are that source; we are just silence, unlimited potential, space and creative energy unfolding. This recognition brings increasingly deeper joy, freedom and compassion. It brings immersion in the unconditional love which is the natural state of our true Self.

2

WEB OF KARMA

There are many ways we can view our existence here on earth. How we see our life, of course, is greatly influenced by our family background, religious upbringing, education, and social circumstances, as well as by our unique inborn personal talents and tendencies. Based on a combination of these factors, we might see life in a variety of not so uplifting ways: for example as a totally random and scientific event, or as something we obviously deserve simply because we are here. Other not uplifting possibilities include seeing it as punishment from a higher power, or as suffering caused by parents, family, and/or societal circumstances.

All these and similar ways of looking at life have their naturally constricting consequences. In order to get beyond the limiting circumstances and conditioning indicated by these examples, it is necessary to look more deeply within ourselves in order to find a more constructive way to relate to the fact that we are here. If we can manage to shift our view away from the kind of attitude described in the examples above and instead begin to see life as a precious gift, as something to be grateful for, and as something to give ourselves selflessly to in a variety of ways, then the possibility of inner growth begins to open up. With such an attitude, life can be a precious opportunity for improvement, joy, and freedom, both for ourselves and for others we come in contact with.

The alternative choices are not conducive to inner growth. If we look upon life as an accidental event or a strictly scientific phenomenon, it tends to become marked by materialism, emotional distance, and skepticism toward anything that cannot be proven through empirical research and intellectual reasoning. This attitude makes it very hard, if not impossible, to recognize and experience a deeper source behind existence. The same is true if we feel that we are locked into being a member of a special group, be it religious, social, national, racial or any other. This view causes life to become, to some degree at least, a battle to prove that our group is special, and that we therefore are right in what we say and do because it represents the norms of our group. We tend to defend ourselves and struggle against others who are not a member of our group and even against ourselves when we fail to measure up to whatever ideals or norms we think belonging to our group demands. Lastly, if we see our life as a kind of curse, punishment, or suffering caused by others, it naturally tends to become a huge disappointment and a struggle against whatever or whomever we think has brought this misery down upon us.

How we view our own existence and that of others, the attitude we have toward the fundamental mystery of life, has everything to do with what our life experience becomes. If we want to free ourselves from being stuck in these learned perspectives and their negative consequences, the first thing we need to do is admit to ourselves the consequences of being stuck in such attitudes. Then we need to consciously begin to open up to another viewpoint. From there, we need to work within ourselves to maintain and expand that openness.

As human beings we choose, unconsciously or unconsciously, how to view our life. We choose to give it meaning or not. This is a responsibility we have to take. It does not mean that we need to feel guilty about the influences, in the form of rewards and traumas that have shaped us along the way. It just means that we must recognize the need for a change in how we relate to life. We need to realize that a deeper openness towards the core of life is necessary. If we wish to grow spiritually, making excuses for being stuck in a view of life that does not promote uplifting our life experience is not beneficial. Blaming our circumstances and condition on factors outside ourselves does not help. It just makes the situation worse. If we want a positive change, reaching more deeply into ourselves to find an open attitude, along with some gratitude for the basic opportunity provided by the fact that we are alive, is an excellent start.

A sure way to free ourselves from being stuck in tensions, blocks, negative patterns and traumas, is to contact and immerse ourselves in the life force at the core of being, where no problems exist. Consciously reaching for this dimension inside ourselves is the first step on the road to spiritual growth and freedom from the web of karma. We have been given, as a gift of life, the willpower to choose what we focus on at all times, regardless of our individual circumstances. This willpower can be used to either become more deeply entangled in tensions, limiting patterns, and negative attitudes, or it can be used to consciously work to free ourselves. By choosing the latter, we express value for the life and free choice we have been given.

Chasing and Clinging

Every society has its patterns that form and bind its members. Modern Western society is becoming ever more marked by materialism and selfish individualism. People want to have their cake and eat it too. For many people life is primarily a chase after money, cars, houses, careers, success, power, relationships, sex, etc., or life is disappointment over not having enough of these things. With a materialistic and selfish attitude, people tend to chase after things, cling to what they get hold of, and then become disappointed about the things they don not get or have. When circumstances change, the tendency is to become distraught. When chasing and clinging dominate our awareness—when achieving, grabbing, and holding on to things is perceived as the primary goal and purpose of our lives—then we are caught and limited by our own desires and life situations. It is as if a veil descends upon us and prevents us from seeing deeper possibilities in ourselves and our surroundings.

If we carefully observe our life experience over time, we may discover that nothing we chase after and cling to can actually bring us lasting joy and well-being. There is never enough of that which does not fully satisfy. Life does not quite seem fully satisfying and meaningful even though we may finally have been promoted at work, bought the big house we wanted, found the relationship of our dreams, and produced the children we desired. Things rarely turn out quite the way we imagined or wanted; at least, they do not usually stay the way we would like for very long. A sense that something is still missing, an underlying anxiety, a feeling of emptiness, or an experience of conflict and separateness usually appears sooner or later for most people. Chasing and clinging to expectations often become disappointment and, in the worst cases, burnout, depression, and illness.

To have or achieve things is not, of course, problematic as such. Nor is it problematic to not have or not achieve certain things. Both what we have and what we are, as well as what we don't have or what we are not, can be experienced as natural aspects of life as a whole, with all its joys and sorrows. It is not what we have or do not have but how we relate to what we have and do not have that is decisive when it comes to the quality of our life experience. It is the attitude of chasing and clinging to expectations that is problematic. The karma theory says that as a human being, we cannot avoid the effect of our actions, and that we cannot avoid action itself. According to the theory, "righteous retribution" is one of life's fundamental laws. For example, if for selfish motives I do something unjust to another person, the law of karma causes some effect to return to me, sooner or later, in some form or other. Of course, this theory is impossible to test and verify scientifically. Its truth can be recognized, however, through inner reflection and spiritual practice (*sadhana*).

A fundamental tenet of the Bible says that "you reap as you sow". The same concept, called the karma theory, appears in Eastern traditions.2 The theory explains the world as an endless chain of cause and effect. In this view, all manifestation consists of an integrated network of parts that are always in a state of change and never separate from, or in essence different from, the whole. This underlying whole is called the Self.

The Self with a capital 'S' is the core of being. It is beyond time and space and at the same time it is everything that exists within time and space. It is the limitless pure awareness that contains all that has existed, does exist, and will exist. It is the root cause and essence of everything that is manifest. As human beings, we *are* essentially this Self. It is our fundamental potential and life force. Everything springs forth from this Self, is maintained by it in time and space, and then dissolves back into it.

The fundamental energy of the Self manifests as increasingly complex vibrations and combinations of waves, forming infinitely complex networks of galaxies, solar systems, physical creatures, and potentially universes other than ours, without ever losing its essence. As this energy unfolds as us, human beings with physical, mental, and emotional bodies, it becomes all our thoughts, feelings, reactions, and actions. On the most subtle plane, the energy vibrates in us as Kundalini. In later chapters, we will return to and further explore the philosophical tradition behind this way of explaining our existence.

We can talk about two types of karma: past and future. Our individual past karma is built into us in the form of *samskaras*, which are scars, traces, or impressions from past actions and experiences. All that we have done and experienced in the past, both in this life and previous lives, remain as traces, or scars, in our psychic body with its subtle energy centers (chakras). These scars and traces influence our physical, mental, and emotional lives. From scars and traces, personal tendencies and patterns spring forth, inviting more entanglement in limitations and conflicts. How we relate to and react to these tendencies and patterns determines, to a large extent, what our future karma becomes.

One example of a karmic trace might be a strong tendency in a person to react negatively whenever someone shows interest in getting closer to him or her. The person with this kind of karmic trace may have very low self esteem due to difficult experiences with family and/or social interaction. As a result, anxiety, pain, or anger may be triggered whenever another person tries to get too close. The response will then be either to pull back or to say or do something that creates a conflict and thus destroys the possibility for closeness or intimacy. The person showing interest may be fully open to and capable of becoming a loyal and positive friend, colleague, boss, teacher, student, lover, spouse, or whatever. He or she might have both the capacity and willingness to add many positive influences and experiences to the life of the person with this karmic trace. Unfortunately, the person with this trace is unable to open to and receive what this situation could potentially offer.

This example represents one of a multitude of possible reactions which have their root cause in karmic traces. In this case, the fact that the person has been betrayed or abandoned in one or more close relationships in this or possibly previous life causes the pain and anger connected with that experience to remain lodged in the person's psychic system. That causes the present to be weighed down by the psychic baggage of the past, even though that baggage has nothing to do with the reality of the present situation. The unresolved, undigested past is controlling the present. Karma rules one's thoughts, emotional reactions, and actions in such a way that the possibilities of the present become greatly limited.

Other karmic traces and scars can form when a person grows up under poor and/or difficult circumstances. It might be in a society where many people perform unethical and illegal acts in order to survive and get ahead. This can cause a person to become accustomed to such acts and absorb them as common and therefore acceptable and natural. Over time, a karmic scar or trace is formed that rules the person's thoughts, reactions, and actions. The person might develop a tendency to grab for him- or herself as many things as possible, regardless of what negative consequences the grabbing might have for others. Even if the person eventually moves to a different society with totally different social rules and expectations (which is quite common in the world today), his or her karmic traces and scars can make it difficult to function and be accepted. What was generally necessary and acceptable in the former society may be far outside the acceptable boundaries of the new society.

From a spiritual perspective, the point is not that a person in such a situation should strive to replace the scars from the old society with the conventions of the new one. The point is to be freed from all such conventions and scars. That means not being caught up in or in opposition to them. The new conventions one meets in a new society are most likely also limiting, though in a different way than those of the former one, and the new ones will leave new scars if one gets locked into them. For example, the new society might be marked by a strong underlying prejudice against individuals from other cultures. This prejudice may be rooted in relatively recent negative experiences with people from other places, or it may be a general suspiciousness toward all "outsiders" due to isolation from or conflicts with the surrounding world over centuries. Such experiences tend to become a common karmic scar for members of the society, a common tendency to prejudge. In this case too, the past is allowed to severely limit the here and now, as well as the future. Those who are controlled by such a background cannot see real individual features and common humanity in people they are not familiar with. Blinded by karmic traces, their experience with rules, patterns, and social conventions have become locked in their psychic system, creating difficulties and conflicts.

It is also quite common for many people to be stuck in karmic traces even though everything on the surface may look quite normal, even very good and successful by societal standards. In many cases, material and practical aspects are fine or even great. People who may be thought of as quite normal or even way above normal in many ways can still be stuck in the limitations of being caught in the web of karma. For example, they may be quite caught in selfishness and superficiality. The cause of this may be a lack of love, effective guidance, inspiration and positive example while growing up. It may be that such people appear on the surface to function well in family and society, yet various underlying karmic traces may cause them to be arrogant, to take other people for granted, to be unnaturally jealous, to be quite selfish, to lack compassion, to be rather unfeeling, and so on. Though most of these traces are hidden beneath the conscious and at first glance visible surface, the traces tend to have a subtle and powerful long term effect on the direction of life. Without an awareness that something deeper exists below the conscious surface, people often get stuck in the limitations of a rather superficial and egocentric life.

It is necessary to respect societal rules and conventions, and to recognize and accept that karmic traces and scars may be the root of rules and conventions that do not seem flexible and compassionate. That is not, however, the same as allowing ourselves to be stuck in rules and conventions. It is possible to respect rules and conventions without allowing our heart to close. It is possible to free ourselves from being caught in or in violent opposition to such rules and conventions. It is possible to avoid the need to react from an inner state limited by the past. It is possible to liberate ourselves from that tendency. This possibility is our main theme, and we will return to it throughout the rest of the book.

The means of freeing ourselves from the past lies in awakening and being immersed in a state of pure awareness, in contact with the essence, the energy at the heart of it all. This means that we observe, from a non-attached witness perspective, our own reactions to life circumstances. We gradually discover our underlying tendencies, blocks, and conventions, i.e. our karmic traces. In a state of open non-judging witnessing, we can consciously let go of the need to react based on conventions and karmic scars. This will dissolve the binding effect of these things. We find that we no longer have to respond with chasing, attacking, clinging, or self-rejection. We no longer have to contribute to the creation of conflicts and difficulties for ourselves and others. We find that through a simple, internally focused awareness, we are free to think, feel, and act from our deepest common humanity rather than from our more superficial and selfish features.

That deeper inner state may also have a subtle but powerful positive effect on social rules and patterns. If enough people become anchored in it, chances are there would be some positive influence on what is for the long term good of humanity. When enough individuals are able to go more deeply within themselves, beyond thoughts, reactions, and behavior patterns, social patterns and rules can begin to change for the better due to the uplifting influence of contact with the Self. Going deeper than conventions and karmic scars, of course, requires structured, continual, internal work over time.

In addition to karmic scars that stem from personally challenging experiences in this life, there are also other traces that do not seem to originate from our current lifetime. It may, therefore, be logical to think that these come from a former life, or from previous generations' experiences. Human beings are all born with a variety of different tendencies. It may be that someone has claustrophobia when stepping into a small, cramped room or is not able to enter an elevator, and that the cause of this may not be traceable to any event or events in this life.

The point of being aware of karmic scars is not to identify where they come from. Rather, it is to reduce or, preferably, to totally dissolve their negative impact on the present and future. As human beings we have the possibility of attaining this. By freeing the energy that lies frozen in karmic scars, life can become freer, richer, and more deeply satisfying. We can prevent further development and reinforcement of negative karma and achieve a great degree of positive influence over our future life experience.

Illusions

In addition to the karmic scars that hinder our life, there are also elements deep in our psychic system that constitutes a liberated unfolding of the deeper will of the Self. This is our unrealized potential, the natural expression of the person we are at the deepest level, that which is most in tune with the universal Self. As we continue to liberate ourselves from the constricting effects of karmic traces, our natural talents and potential are allowed to unfold more and more from within us. This springs from the essence of our being in order to realize our purpose in this life. It can create challenges for us, but in contrast to reactions based on locked-in karmic scars, the unfolding has a natural force and flow that can deeply fulfill us. It may be that we have a natural calling or ability to serve in some vocation or other, or in a particular social role, sport, or artistic endeavor.

In order to nurture this natural unfolding, it is essential to provide nourishment to the inner energy system. Latent talents and abilities are embedded as seeds of pure potential in the core of our being. Regularly paying attention to our core being, giving it our conscious focus and wish, this natural unfolding happens. This attention is like watering the seeds of our being. In the process, we let go of chasing, clinging and expectations, including habitual reactions to locked-in karmic scars and illusions, elements that drain us of vital energy.

People often chase and cling to draining illusions instead of feeding their core reality. An example would be a tendency to always incorrectly judge oneself as inept at some activity or other, despite the fact that one actually has great potential in that particular area. If, instead of feeding this illusion, the person would open up to the deeper potential of the Self, natural abilities and opportunities could be discovered. Illusions would be revealed as such, and true potential could be realized.

Another example of an illusion is to always react in opposition to everything and everyone, even though no one is attacking. Or a person may tend to always take it for granted that he or she is better at something or other than a person from another societal background or of a different skin color than his or her own, despite the fact that this is not necessarily the case. If the ego has an inflated tendency to want to achieve something big in some field or other, this can also be an illusion. It may be that one believes one has capabilities and a natural call to something, but that it is not a reality. In such a case, one only creates difficulties for oneself by striving in just that direction. One ends up banging on doors that will never open and at some point, it is best to stop feeding that illusion.

Another tendency that is prevalent today is to measure oneself against idealized physical beauty and accomplishments presented in the social media. These pictures and descriptions tend to be greatly exaggerated social ideals that most people cannot and need not realize. For most of us these ideals are basically illusions that we might waste a lot of effort and attention striving towards.

Life is the best teacher in terms of revealing our true callings, our real capabilities, and our most natural fate, i.e. that which is in tune with the natural flow of the Self. If we think we have a huge talent in some area or other but never manage to qualify for any real accomplishment in that area, we must sooner or later accept that this is not a real calling or possibility for our creative engagement. To chase after something we desire very much beyond a certain point despite consistent signs that it is not going to materialize is to throw away our life force on an illusion.

Similarly, if we are possessed by the idea that to be married is the only way to live while at the same time living in a marriage that is not working at all, and if we continue to give of ourselves to this malfunctioning marriage without seeking improvement or dissolution, then we are investing in a hindering illusion rather than a potentially fulfilling reality. The opposite can also represent an illusion. If we get out of a marriage or situation of commitment as soon as it becomes more challenging than expected, that may be based on the illusion that it is never worth-while to work through difficulties in order to gain a deeper relationship with a person or situation we have made a commitment to. The tendency to get out too quickly because there are so many other tempting solutions that seem better or easier is very prevalent in today's society. The grass often seems greener on the other side, tempting us to move before having given an existing challenge a real chance to resolve itself.

Tensions

What we chase after and cling to becomes our web of karma. This all stems from what is called the "biological imperatives," embedded within all human beings at birth: to survive and reproduce. Social patterns, and in our time the social media, build on these imperatives in different ways to create an increasingly complex web of desires, which, over time, form deep karmic scars. To the extent that we relate to life mainly as chasing and clinging, we are doomed to experience increased stress, disappointment, and suffering. The more we chase after and cling to expectations, the more we increase our karmic difficulties and tensions. It is a negative cycle that feeds on itself.

As mentioned in the first chapter, tension is like an inner ice, like a frozen life force. It is experienced as internal tightness, coldness, imbalance, discomfort, or numbness. Over time, unresolved tension tends to result in serious fatigue, conflict, illness, and/or burnout. We gradually become less and less confident and capable on many levels, mentally, emotionally, and physically. Tension restricts our ability to think, feel, and act freely. Our range of outlook, choice, and movement becomes narrower. Our physical health is negatively affected. We become more limited, less happy, and less creative people.

Tension slowly accumulates over the years and becomes locked within layers of physical and psychic tissues. The energy system (chakras) and the creative flow in the body are gradually blocked. In this way, we slowly but surely become constrained by chasing after and clinging to things that really cannot satisfy us deeply, but that we have been programmed to believe are essential. The web of karma catches us and entangles us more and more. This is the usual condition for most human beings. A great many people thus miss the key challenge and possibility life has to offer: to awaken awareness of the fundamental life force and to become immersed in the natural unfolding of this force.

Based on biological imperatives, the ego comprises many layers of mental, emotional, and behavioral patterns that are useful for survival and reproduction. However, these same patterns also create blocks, illusions, tensions, and constraints that interfere with the experience and unfolding of the fundamental life force. Ego development occurs primarily through feedback from family and community, and it is, for the most part, intended to make us successful at surviving and reproducing, in other words, to be good citizens. This is natural and important to a certain extent in our development, and in order for society to function efficiently. However, from a spiritual viewpoint, it is problematic when over time the ego focus, which is almost exclusively concerned with taking, getting, and having, becomes so strong that it seriously hinders us from experiencing something deeper and finer in and around us. We become so entrenched in our relatively superficial concerns that we have neither the interest nor the time for anything else. That which helps satisfy our biological imperatives at some point becomes a huge obstacle, thwarting our spiritual growth, liberation, and deep, long-lasting well-being. In our eagerness to comply with the goals of our biology and ego, we destroy the possibility of authentic inner experience and growth.

Imbalance

For many centuries most people, especially in Western societies, have defined and experienced themselves primarily in terms of mental constructs and ideologies. That has created a certain imbalance both on an individual level, with mental, emotional, and physical suffering experienced through a sense of separation, self-denial, depression, anger, and prejudices, and on a societal level through conflicts, violence, and war.

The French philosopher Descartes said in the 1600s that *"I think therefore I am."* This philosophy was a reaction against too much emphasis on the church and its dogmas. It placed emphasis on rational thinking rather than worship and feelings guided by religion. In so doing, it helped to lay the foundation for the mechanistic, individualistic, and reductionist philosophy that continues to characterize the West today. The philosophy became the basis for the industrialization and technology development that has taken place over the last few centuries. In line with this philosophy, until recent scientific developments refuted it, the physical universe was viewed as a limited mechanism composed of distinct parts. The same view gradually colored the perception of what it means to be a human being.

Modern Western medicine, for example, has a tendency to view the human body as a *thing* made up of separate parts. Therefore, it is often difficult for a medical specialist to relate to parts of a patient's physiology that are outside the specialist's area of expertise. Departments and parts rule, not awareness of the whole. In addition, this mechanistic view also holds that only what can be observed with the human senses, and that which can be measured, is accepted as true reality. This excludes viewing a human being as a process connected with universal, unlimited awareness. This mechanistic outlook stands in sharp contrast to the East's age-old outlook, exemplified by Eastern treatment methods which view the body as a conscious process and holistic presence, with pressure points or other subtle factors that can be stimulated to restore the balance, health, and well-being of the whole so that the entire process unfolds more fully and naturally. The focus is on stimulating an increased flow of energy throughout the system so that the inherent healing ability of the person kicks in.

In the Tantric tradition of Kashmir Shaivism, which we shall explore in more detail in a later chapter, the understanding of reality is the opposite of what has characterized the West in recent centuries. The perception of reality in this tradition has, to a large extent, developed through a process of inner meditative practice that made it possible for practitioners to discover that there is, at the core of being, an underlying Consciousness with unlimited potential and power. Contrary to Descarte's declaration, this experience told them that "I am, therefore, I think." They saw that awareness of being comes first, and that this dimension is without any limits. They saw that all physical, mental, and emotional phenomena arise, sustain themselves for a time, and then dissolve, all within that limitless awareness. They saw that first we *are*, and then we *think*. Sartre, Camus, and other existentialists began to touch on this in the mid-1900s. They wrote from a perspective of *being*, an existential awareness that lies deeper than our thoughts and programmed responses. Like the Tantric practitioners of more than a thousand years ago, they concluded that the fundamental sense of being here and now is more basic and powerful than any conceptual activity, mental construct, or ideology.

*

As one of my meditation students said after a few years of practice, "*You meet yourself in the door.*" What we usually first meet in ourselves when we turn our attention inward is our ego patterns. In other words, we come face-to-face with our tendencies, thoughts, scars, reactions, tensions, illusions, and blocks. We meet our identity and all the limitations connected with it. We meet everything we have to let go of in order to be immersed in the Self.

In business, entertainment, education, and other venues we can relatively easily see a difference between those who are very locked in ego focus and those who are more open to a deeper and broader reality. Those who are very entrenched in their ego often seem overly controlling, more dominating, manipulative, and superficial, or filled with conflict, repression, and suffering. There seems to be less common humanity and compassion behind what they say and do. Those who are more connected with a deeper reality, on the other hand, seem less selfish and better able to communicate and act from a more humane, open, and compassionate awareness.

It is fully possible, in all arenas, to be in contact with the fundamental life force while playing a role in society. Even if we have an important position, we can still be in contact with the energy of the Self as we act out whatever the position calls for. As we play out our natural roles in life, we can choose to relate from the deepest and most common humanity in ourselves as we interact with others.

In relating to others, the more entrenched the egos that confront us in the course of our daily activities are, in any role, the more energy is actually available to us. If we consciously hold our awareness open and free from judgment, and if we refrain from reacting negatively, then we allow the effect of the ego in that particular situation to dissolve. It becomes digestible energy for us, which, when circulated through our psychic system, broadens our horizon, causing us to become more open and wiser human beings. For example, the abundance of tension, imbalance and ego found in a gigantic city like New York provides a colossal reservoir of potential energy flow. To the degree that we succeed in focusing on what lies at the core of the people and situations we come in contact with, we gain access to the fundamental energy buried there. However, this requires deep immersion in the Self, and a lot of inner work.

The ego lives by reacting and by getting others to react. When we respond from ego, the outcome is always more limited than when we act consciously, in a state of openness, in contact with the Self. Sooner or later ego reactions lead to attacks on others, conflicts, and/or attacks on ourselves. Whether we react based on an identity that says that we are better than everyone else, or based on an identity that says that we are worth less than everyone else, ego is the guiding force in both cases. Both reactions are based on a clinging to the limitations of ego. Often, these two extremes manifest in the same person at different times and in different situations. All this has nothing to do with the deeper reality of life.

*

The means of freeing ourselves from the web of karma lies in awakening and being immersed in a state of pure awareness, in contact with the essence, the energy at the core of it all. That means that we are in a state where we observe, with our witness awareness, our own reactions, feelings, thoughts, and actions. To the extent that we open to it, this witness awareness, and the discovery of the subtle energy that unfolds there, is our inner teacher. It is a pure inner gaze of awareness.

With a non-attached perspective, we gradually discover the tendencies, blocks, and patterns that we are locked in. This is not something to feelguilty about, but it can reveal clearly to us what to work on. We can then, perhaps inspired, nourished and guided by a teacher, consciously let go of the need to react based on negative patterns and karmic limitations. This letting go will dissolve the binding effect of these patterns and limitations. It moves our awareness into the unknown, into an open boundless state. This has a tendency to bring out fear and resistance. By working through this inner obstacle, we find that we no longer have to respond with chasing, attacking, clinging, or self-rejection. We no longer contribute to the creation of conflicts and difficulties for ourselves and others. We find that through a simple, inner awareness we are free to think, feel, and act from our deepest common humanity rather than from our more superficial features.

We can learn from our experiences by taking life's feedback to heart. In fact, the reason we attract challenging situations and react to them the way we do is to learn certain lessons. If we open up and look carefully from a state of non-attachment, the difference between reality and illusion in all situations becomes clarified over time. The voice of the Self speaks through our life. To the extent that we listen and are aligned with that deepest part of ourselves, we are uplifted. To the extent that we stay entangled in ego and illusions, we descend into some combination of tension, repression, denial, separation, depression, and conflict.

Karma is like an infinite web. It is easy to get caught in but very difficult to become free of. We all become caught and entangled in our own unique way. Whether we are conscious of it or not, and whether we greatly resist it or not, we always end up doing what is natural for us: we move. Movement and action are basic features of human life and the universe, and it cannot be avoided. Resistance to movement is also a kind of movement in that it drains us of energy.

Our inner state as we move is critical as to the outcome in relation to the web of karma. With every move or action, we necessarily cause a change in our relationship to our karmic web. Our motive and inner state are what determine whether an action further entangles us and creates more karma, or, if we act from a free, open state, will lift us above the level of karma, thus untangling us from it. It is impossible to start either life or spiritual work outside the web of karma. It is also impossible to be completely separated from it at any time. Fortunately, it is possible to immerse ourselves in the Self and transform the web from something that catches us to something that uplifts us.

Solution

When we seriously turn our attention within and observe ourselves in a non-attached and open attitude, we gradually see what kind of ego-identity we are caught in. We see our patterns, scars, illusions, tensions, and blocks, and we begin to see more clearly the limiting thoughts and reactive patterns in ourselves. We become aware of what creates separation, conflict, depression, and self-denial, and thus makes us less happy than would otherwise be possible. If, along with this realization, we consciously refrain from reacting to what we see and just gratefully let go while staying focused on the fundamental energy flow, then the patterns and blocks begin to dissolve. Our inner gaze of awareness sees the ego in the form of karmic scars, illusions, and tensions as these reveal themselves. Over time, this gaze has the strength to melt and transform everything, even our most powerful patterns.

To let go is simply a matter of shifting awareness away from ego focus to an open state of grateful witnessing. The techniques of the Rising Energy Practice are designed to accomplish that, and it can slowly be learned by application over time. Through regular deep practice, it becomes clear that no tension or pattern can survive in an open state of grateful witnessing.

As mentioned earlier, our inner gaze of awareness is our inner spiritual teacher. It can help liberate us (and others, when it becomes powerful enough) from patterns and tensions. The same patterns and tensions may, of course, emerge again in the future. This means we must be vigilant and say, "no, thank you," to the tensions and limiting patterns over and over again, while maintaining our attention on the deeper reality. This is the continuous, lifelong inner practice that needs to be done in order to free ourselves and to help others in the liberation process. It's necessary to let go and let go and let go.

If we refrain from taking the ego-bait set out by people and situations around us by not reacting to it, we succeed in not giving nourishment to the ego game. We do not reinforce the ego patterns further. We have a choice every moment in terms of how we respond to what we confront in the form of communication and action from others, and within ourselves, in the form of our reactions to various situations. Even if someone says or does something with the intention of harming us, we do not have to react outwardly and thereby throw fuel on the fire. Instead, we can draw our energy inside and go directly to the underlying awareness. We can focus on the breath, the energy flow in the chakra system, and on the simple awareness at the core of it all.

There is a liberating joy in the experience of the fundamental life force inside us. The energy tingles in the hand when we focus attention and feel into it. It opens like a flower in the heart center when we focus there, and likewise in the other chakras. Champagne bubbles or powerful waves move up the spine when as the Kundalini energy unfolds, rising up to the top of the head. It is no longer as interesting to analyze ego-related constraints when we have a simple inner working method and a contact that can dissolve these restraints.

The solution, which we now have briefly looked at and which we will further expand on in later chapters, is to take refuge in the pure awareness that is the ground of everything. This can be experienced as a simple conscious and grateful presence. The solution lies not in attempting to fix something we perceive as a problem or illusion only through analysis of where or how it originated, or by brainstorming for improvement ideas. The point is not to condemn our own thoughts, reactions, or actions, or those of others. The solution is not to wallow in guilt over what we have done wrong or over the fact that we have had or are having difficulties in life. The solution is simply to acknowledge our state while at the same time letting go of all guilt, problematic thinking, and reacting. It is to move our awareness from focus on tension, analysis and worries into an open grateful witnessing. This may sound like an oversimplification, but it is not necessarily easy. It requires regular, deep inner practice over time. Through pure awareness we come in contact with the deepest part of ourselves, where no problems exist. There is only a simple presence and gratitude for life.

3

GROWTH

If we manage to relate to life as a gift, we might ask ourselves: *"What is the purpose of this gift? What is the meaning of life here on earth?"* The Tantric tradition described in Kashmir Shaivism says that the meaning of this life is to grow in recognition of the Self, of who we really are.

The energy that we deliberately ingest through our life is fuel for our inner growth. When we deliberately circulate this energy through the internal energy system in the body, it rises to the top of the head and becomes a reservoir that eventually overflows and gives off fine nourishment in the brain. In Eastern art, swelling or small bumps at the top of the head of the depicted divine figure are often seen; this shows the collection of energy that occurs through inner practice and realization. The universal energy has risen to the top of the head and has become wisdom and compassion.

If we are not in contact with the fundamental energy but instead stuck in and controlled by ego, then everything in life is, as previously noted, nothing but a kind of business. When we relate to life this way, we tend to want to keep an account of everything, and we tend to hold back and be suspicious and cautious. Lust, greed, expectations, frustration, disappointment, stress, and tension are in control. This does not allow for a free flow and exchange of energy.

In contrast, an attitude rooted in the wish for inner growth allows the heart and energy system to open up so the fundamental energy can awaken and unfold in our awareness. Everything then appears for the sake of inner nourishment, without the need for accounting and tension. To the extent that we choose to see life this way, as an energy flow rather than a series of transactions requiring accounting, we always get back more than we give, in the form of transformative and uplifting inner experience.

To grow inside is to become more and more immersed and rooted in an internal state that is free from viewing life as business, free from accounting, and free from tension in the body, mind, and emotions. It is to let our awareness deepen so that we have contact with finer energy dimensions. The process is to gather this energy and bring it through our internal system. As we absorb and digest it, inner transformation occurs.

Inner growth happens by letting go of thoughts, prejudices, scars, judgments, expectations, blocks, illusions, and patterns associated with ego. These limitations often make life very challenging here and now and are expressed in the form of anxiety, loneliness, anger, self-pity, guilt, conflicts, and/or a feeling of separation. When we are stuck in ego, the self with a small 's', our life sooner or later becomes full of problems. In contrast, when we become immersed in the Self with a capital 'S', we go deeper than ego-related issues and are, in our life here and now, united with the deeper and true core reality. We can then experience a state that may be called uplifted or transcendent, in the sense that energy and unconditional well-being saturate our awareness. We no longer feel compelled to worry every day about natural ups and down, including the fact that death will inevitably come. We get used to being in an open state that can go through cycles of letting go and being reborn. To the extent that we are able to stay in touch with this open state in everyday life, we are greatly helped to openly encounter whatever comes, even as the physical body dissolves. We understand that life and death are two sides of the same coin, two sides of the same fundamental universal potential and energy.

Horizontal and Vertical

The terms "horizontal" and "vertical" have been used to describe different dimensions of inner growth.3 All patterns are horizontal, meaning that they have form, whether coarse or subtle, and these forms represent our mental and emotional clinging. When we start the growth process, the patterns we are stuck in are usually rather coarse and basic. As we grow, these coarse patterns dissolve, and more subtle patterns take form and become visible. All patterns are horizontal, regardless of how coarse or subtle they are, in that they exist parallel to the surface of the earth. The densest and coarsest patterns lie closest to the earth; finer patterns exist in increasingly higher levels of the atmosphere according to their vibration frequency.

In contrast to the horizontal, the vertical dimension represents the fundamental energy unfolding that is the source of all horizontal manifestation, and that awakens in our awareness through inner practice. The vertical is the formless dimension; it is the essence of all patterns and forms that continuously unfold, are sustained for a time, and then dissolve. In order not to become lost and stuck in the form and tension of this process, we continuously open to and immerse ourselves in the vertical dimension. We can ride this dimension through all tension, patterns and forms. We can continuously let go of and digest all materiality, transforming it into the fuel we need to ascend into finer levels of awareness and experience. As we learn to master this process, inner growth accelerates.

It is through the vertical dimension of pure creative energy that we make contact with Shiva, pure Consciousness, that which in modern science is called, among other things, the *"psi-field"*.4 This ocean of infinite potential is beyond time and space. It is, according to Laszlo and other scientist, aligned with the Shiva concept of ancient Eastern texts. Laszlo describes, from the modern scientific perspective, a boundless *"meta-verse"* that *"in-forms,"* meaning it gives form to all that exists, has existed, and ever will exist, from the subtlest vibration to the densest physical form.

When we, through the vertical dimension, come in contact with Shiva, with that which lies deeper than time and space, we open ourselves to receive *"in-formation"* that transforms us from the density close to the earth to the subtler existence of finer levels. We open to receive nourishing vibrations from higher dimensions.

Waking Up

In the first weeks that I participated in the Open Eyes meditation that my teacher Rudi held, I had no idea what he meant by the term "energy flow." I felt completely welcome and accepted. Sometimes I saw other practitioners move spontaneously or make sounds as if they were experiencing something deep inside, but I did not experience anything special. I was mainly aware of my own insecurity and anxiety. I became increasingly conscious of my own tension and constriction in the heart area, and it was difficult to feel any expansion or energy flow there. It was also difficult to bring my attention deeper into the chakra system. Still, I continued to work at the practice. I had an intuitive trust in Rudi and was convinced that what he had taught me would, sooner or later, bring about some kind of breakthrough.

In the course of the first months with Rudi, after a period of hard physical labor around his NYC ashram, this breakthrough became a reality. During meditation, I breathed deeply into the heart center, held my breath and focus there, and asked to feel a strong expansion. Without warning, my whole being suddenly dissolved into the heart center and exploded there in a million tiny fragments of light. Powerful waves of warmth shot up my spine at the same time, causing some very strong "kriyas" (spontaneous bodily movements).

The only way I could interpret this experience was that the love and energy that flowed through the contact and inner effort had reached a new level in me, melting solid blocks inside and releasing the energy trapped in them. It was as if large, inner blocks of ice simply melted, became water and steam, and then were transformed into powerful energy. Following this explosive energetic experience, total stillness and peace emerged from deep within me. I was very grateful, as something deep and powerful that had been dormant had come alive in my awareness. I continued to have similar strong experiences for many years after that.

Energy Flow

Dramatic spontaneous bodily movements *(kriyas)* are not necessarily something everyone experiences as a result of this practice. Nor are they something one should especially seek in the course of the transformation process. An individual's process can be much less dramatic than what I experienced without thereby being any less significant. How the process unfolds within each person depends on the blocks and psychic scars that exist in the system and on how deeply one lets go then and there. For most people, some form or other of kriyas happen as tension is released. Even though these movements may be very mild, they can be experienced as the dissolution of tension and as a stronger flow of energy in the system.

For me, these relatively explosive experiences provided an early indication that what I felt was not just theory but something extremely powerful and very real. What I experienced was clearly a living energy. I did not, of course, understand exactly what was happening to me, and there were elements of both fear and thrill in it. It was like jumping from a high cliff without knowing where or how I would land.

The result of such experiences is simply an expanded recognition of the conscious power that is the fundamental cause of being. From this emerges an experience of dynamic stillness, a simple presence marked by deep joy and gratitude for being alive, for being able to breathe and feel a kind of boundless connection with life. Energy that before was crystallized in specific blocks, patterns and tensions, is now liberated and in a state of free flow. In this transaction, the psychic mechanism is transformed. Awareness is totally different. Possibilities for self-expression expand greatly. Creative energy is released inside and spreads out as an uplifting vibration towards everyone and everything we meet. Inner ice turns to flow; gradually we become grounded in an experience of inner glow, joy, peace, and power.

As tension and inner ice melts, we begin to experience the fundamental energy source behind all existence. We begin to recognize Oneness, in the sense that all people and all existence *are* the same energy we recognize in ourselves, even though most people are not aware of it. This recognition ripens into natural compassion for others as we gradually become unified with the qualities of the Self at our core. We experience dynamic stillness as a living reality.

No Need to Destroy Ego

The web of karma is primarily created through attachment to ego identity. Still, there is nothing wrong with ego. Everyone has an ego. But what we learn to do is what the Indian spiritual teacher Nisargadatta has said: *"You don't have to tear your house down to be free."* 5 House here refers to ego-identity. This identity may be a prison in that it causes us to act out patterns that greatly complicate our life. Still, we do not have to use our meditation practice to try to destroy our ego-identity. That is not the goal. What we want is to not be stuck in the tensions and patterns of our identity. To be free of attachment to the ego-identity that we are imprisoned in, we just have to find a door into the deeper Self. That door can be found by opening up within to a totally open and pure awareness. This can be done in meditation and also while interacting with anything in life.

A most easily accessible door to deeper awareness is found within us in the form of the chakra system. If we have a teacher, that connection can also be used as a doorway to our deeper Self. We bring our attention into the chakras or our connection and instead of judging and despairing, feeling that this world is terrible and that we hate or doubt everybody and our own self, we just ask deeply to open within ourselves. Suddenly, perhaps when we least expect it, the door within us opens wide. We go through this door and suddenly we are in a different state. We might say to ourselves: *"Oh, I'm in a deeper stillness and energy. I can surrender myself into that and it's so nourishing."*

We are now no longer as driven by and caught in our desires, judgments, likes and dislikes as before. We know we have this door into a deeper state. To be able to enter through this door is really wonderful. It is transforming and liberating. Through practice we can learn how to go in and out of it at will, at any time. When difficult challenges come, we know where to go. When we need to attract and activate creative energy for what we want in life, we know where to place our attention. We do not have to stay and fight with every situation or get more and more under it. We do not have to judge the situation, other people or ourselves. We work at it, practice, dig for the deeper state, wish for it, and persevere even if it takes quite some time to open inside. If we persist, the door gradually opens. Eventually, we are able to open it at will and have momentary experiences of that deeper state whenever we need it. Over time, through inner work, we can become totally immersed in that state.

Even when we are sitting in a difficult meeting at work, or in a difficult interaction with a partner, family or friend, we can be present in our ego identity while at the same time being connected with the deeper Self. It is not impossible to do that. We learn the process and become convinced that we can do it when it counts the most. Over time our awareness and life experience are totally transformed.

Joy and Strength

How can we transform stress and worry into joy and strength? To be in is a state of repression and denial is most challenging. This is when we do not really acknowledge our feelings but instead sweep things under the carpet, which is a tendency many people have. The difficulty with repression and denial is that we hardly ever deal with anything. We can end up with a sense of being completely out of touch with our feelings. Life seems flat and lifeless, and not very fulfilling. We are not really allowing ourselves to express what is in our heart.

Some time back a study was done into what dying people felt that they regretted most. A thing high on the list of the people interviewed as they approached death was that they regretted that they had not emphasized the importance of being happier in their life. They implied that happiness is something you choose by giving it your consistent conscious attention. These people regretted that they did not live with enough love and care for their inner life. They regretted placing too much attention on external and material things at the expense of attention on the experience of inner joy.

Life has a lot of challenges for everyone, but there is a way we can prevent an attitude of repression and denial. To consciously turn our attention within and begin working on opening up and allowing ourselves to feel whatever is inside us is a good way to start. Gradually, we can realize that everything we feel, even though it may be quite painful and difficult at times, is fundamentally pure potential and energy flow. This is something we can experience for ourselves through inner practice.

The ego causes repression and denial as well as uncontrolled eruption and indulgence of feelings such as anger, fear and depression. The ego wants to either protect itself through repression and denial or it wants to express itself while only caring for itself. It does not want to face that sometimes feeling anger, sadness, depression or fear is perfectly natural and something we should allow ourselves to fully feel while at the same time re-channeling the energy of the emotions through our inner psychic system. Ego wants to either push our real feelings down because they do not conform to the idea we have in our mind of who we are or it wants to blow off steam by reacting without restraint and self control.

To counteract these ego tendencies requires a conscious inner practice. Instead of pushing real feelings down or allowing them to erupt in expression that only creates tension or conflict, the practice guides us to go into the feelings. It allows us to open to it and dissolve it in our awareness. We can go more deeply into the feeling and just experience it for the energy flow that it truly is. That makes it possible to realize that we really are not limited by the form of our emotions, worries and reactions. Instead, we can experience more deeply the flow of life that they represent. We do not have to identify so much with them but instead allow them to flow within us as energy.

Rising Above Ego

As we feel that we are rising up within ourselves and are above our limitations, we are doing so on the vertical dimension described above. We relate to the vertical and rise on it to awareness beyond our ego identity. Our spine is straight and energy can move along it and rise to the top of the head. In that way, we connect vertically to finer dimensions that can dissolve patterns and refine our system.

Energy rises from the base of the spine through the chakras to the top of the head and the flow cleans up various tendencies, blocks and tensions lodged in the chakras. When we rise and feel that we are above our problems, they become less important. This process creates a new mechanism inside us. Where before there were blockages and negative patterns, there is now a psychic mechanism in which tensions can dissolve and where creative energy can flow.

The deeper flow starts to attract different things in our life, challenges maybe, but also wonderful situations because we are in a better state. We have a deeper and more open and joyful vibration inside. It is a finer and more conscious state than what we were in before. Our surroundings respond to this finer quality. The vibration in the space inside us attracts a finer life experience and new opportunities. If, on the other hand, we are full of ego, what can we attract? Unfortunately, ego awareness tends to attract only more ego awareness. It feeds on itself.

When two egos interact without deeper awareness, there is always a sense of tension and conflict. In contrast, when two people who are both working inside and are open interact, there is a sense of energy flow and common humanity. There is recognition of the basic humanity and Oneness, and there is a sharing of that awareness. What else could be more important? How much money do we want? How much material stuff do we need? There is never enough of that which does not satisfy. The only thing that really satisfies is the deeper state of being one with and sharing awareness of the deeper Self.

When we do the practice and this energy starts to rise, it refines our psychic system by meeting the universal dimension of our being. There is gradual recognition of energy flow and Oneness. The space that we open in our heart is essentially the same as space everywhere. We can pour all our problems into that space and allow them to melt or be ground up into fresh creative energy. Matter is not lost; it is only mysteriously transformed into joy, wisdom and compassion. It's a little like a black whole sucking up all materiality and transforming it into extremely powerful energy flow.

Extending Practice

As we go into a meditation practice, it is very beneficial to extend it into everyday life. When we are in the various situations that usually are full of challenges, tension, stress and distraction, we step back a little bit and have a different experience of the situation. No matter what we are doing, we can take a conscious breath, feel into our heart, and feel the transformation from stuck to opening and energy flow. We can gradually realize that no problem can survive in an open heart. The openness melts the tension of the problem and turns it into energy flow.

When we really feel stuck in a mental, emotional or any other kind of difficulty, we bring it all into our heart. It is a way of getting our "stuff" together and using it as fuel for our inner fire. We bring it all in there. We get centered. We feel how tight it is. Anything we bring our attention to will at first feel tighter. Eventually, if we ask deeply enough and long enough while at the same time letting go, our heart will open wide, allowing the tension and pattern to melt.

As noted earlier, it can open softly or more explosively. It can be felt as a very subtle shift inside, like a subtle opening and energy flow, like a flower opening or like champagne bubbles going up the spine. We can feel a melting of tensions in the chakras and then a kind of joyful energy moving down and finally rising to the top of the head. It flows as a result of our sincere wish and by letting go of attachment. It is not dependent on any external situation. Sometimes the opening can happen with a lot of noise, like a huge iceberg braking up and falling into the ocean. Many different strong and subtle experiences are possible. However it happens, it is quite incredible that this process can be felt again and again.

Glimpses

In our society today, there is growing interest in yoga, alternative treatment methods, and meditation practices. Many people feel an urgent need to liberate themselves from the materialistic and technological focus of modern life. Many have a sensation that there must be something deeper than the more or less superficial and overwhelming daily life they live. Something deeper and finer, a kind of mystical peace and strength, sometimes whispers its promises from beneath the selfish and socially dominated surface. In this way, many people are experiencing a natural pull toward inner growth. But the subtle sensation that there is a deeper potential under the surface is difficult to keep hold of, and even more difficult to get a strong experience of. Therefore, the sensation is often quickly swept under the carpet and forgotten.

To the extent that we open and get a glimpse of the deeper quality beneath the surface, we are in momentary contact with the inherent qualities of the Self: its power, creativity, joy, and energy flow. We get a glimpse of the here and now as existence without limitation, as something much deeper and more profound than all our personal problems. Such glimpses give a taste of liberation, a taste of the fundamental source of our being, a taste of what we really are. Examples of this type of experience can be found in the simple joy of life and natural, playful creativity most of us have encountered as children and at various special peak moments of our adult lives.

Contact with the fundamental life force can be truly uplifting and liberating, while at the same time both frightening and awe-inspiring in its power and boundlessness. After a glimpse of this dimension, it is possible to become scared and flee to the safe, well-known thoughts and patterns we are familiar with, or we can open to the possibility that a burden is beginning to fall from our shoulders, making it easier to breathe and feel joy, gratitude, and creative power. We can reject and run away from the contact or we can become more deeply motivated to further explore this newfound treasure. What is required in order for the latter to happen is maintaining a sustained choice to open to the possibility, and to choose to work regularly with a conscious inner practice.

Going Deeper

In order to enact a profound change in life, choosing to open up to a contact with an inner yearning for something deeper than the more or less superficial aspects of life is necessary. From this longing, we can get in touch with a teacher and practice that can help guide our inner work. Only through a deep contact and practice over time can the most entrenched inner blocks and limitations be dissolved so that the creative power that lies at the core of existence can unfold. As a practitioner, our inner psychic system can be completely transformed over time. Wanting inner growth and liberation demands finding a practice and contact that works, and then to consciously use what is found to the best of our abilities, again and again.

It may be necessary and advisable to take whatever time it takes to find a practice and a teacher we feel we can trust, and that really fit our temperament and needs. However, we cannot remain on an endless search and expect to get very far in terms of inner growth. For one who really wants to grow inside, it is very positive to find a practice to invest serious time and energy in, no matter what else is happening in life. If this is made a priority and we give ourselves to the process in a variety of ways, our whole inner system can be transformed over time.

Inner growth is a process that leads to a total transformation of consciousness. In order to begin such a process and thereby open the possibility of liberation in this lifetime, a sincere wish to grow inside must somehow be generated and then cultivated over time. It is necessary to invest our attention in a radically different way than what is common in modern society. We consciously shift focus away from chasing and clinging to things and instead toward exploring the core within. It represents a totally different sense of the purpose and meaning of life.

4

GUIDANCE

A person who has learned to live in tune with the fundamental energy source at the core of being can help inspire, nourish and guide us in our quest for inner transformation. Through depth of commitment and surrender to the source of being, the creative energy at the core of life, such a person is able to profoundly affect the state of others by inspiring and guiding them in their growth process.

In the Tantric tradition there are certain aspects that, through many generations of practice and contemplation, have emerged as extremely important. One such aspect is, as already mentioned, the importance of contact with a capable guide. In the East, a spiritual guide is traditionally called a guru. The Shiva Sutras, a main text in the Tantric tradition (see Sources), emphatically state that *"the guru is the means."* This is in tune with most Eastern spiritual traditions. In the West the word guide or teacher may be more easily acceptable for most people, since the word guru has received some very negative connotations through scandals and abuse. The word teacher, guide or mentor is, therefore, used interchangeably here to describe a person serving this purpose.

Although it is possible to grow inside without an outer teacher, it is extremely rare to become liberated without such a contact. The reason for this is that the ego needs to be revealed and consciously surrendered through contact with the deeper energetic state of another human being. Without that contact, and the feedback inherent in it, the ego will usually win, feeding on its own patterns and structures.

If our goal is inner growth, it is not wise to close ourselves off from the possibility of receiving nourishment and guidance from a living teacher. Worrying about whether or not a teacher fits into some preconceived idea of how a perfect teacher should look and behave is counterproductive. Our own expectations, prejudices, and socially learned attitudes will then most likely prevent the possibility of inner growth.

A teacher should serve as an example of the state we are seeking. That does not mean we should copy the teacher's personal characteristics, or let ourselves be manipulated or controlled. It simply means that we use the contact to immerse ourselves in the deep state of openness and energy flow that the contact is an invitation to. Especially in the beginning, a teacher is helpful in giving instructions regarding practice methods. Guidance, especially at important crossroads, is also helpful, and so is energetic support and inspiration. A teacher's main function is to help dissolve tension, patterns, and blocks. He or she should challenge ego boundaries and give authentic feedback through presence, words, and actions. In these ways, a teacher is a point of connection to the spiritual dimension of daily life.

It is necessary to rely on our gut feeling with respect to any teacher we come in contact with. This means opening to a deeper level than our expectations, prejudices, and attitudes. These must, as far as possible, be set aside, on trust, so that we can be in a receptive state. As contact with a teacher is established and begins to unfold, it is necessary to have all our senses open and to feel into the situation in order to know whether or not this teacher can provide the deep inner nourishment we need, and whether to trust him or her in the long term and therefore stay connected. It may take a long time to feel into what the contact means, but as soon as we take the step of accepting a teacher into our life as a support and means of inner growth, then it will no longer do to relate to the teacher with constant suspicion. We cannot be full of anxiety about what may or may not happen through the contact. As in other relationships in life, but even more so: we cannot get much out of the relationship if we close our heart and mind to it. Openness, love, and respect are essential.

Doorway

Being connected with a tradition and having a teacher can be of great importance. Anyone who is a real teacher is not interested in controlling us, or getting anything from us. A real teacher is interested in sharing something with us. That is the only reward a teacher can expect for doing the work of helping people who come for guidance and support. Anything else is an illusion and projection of ego-identity. The real reward a teacher can have is to share in other people's experience of their transformation, sharing in others' joy of going through a process similar to what the teacher has gone through. This is wonderful. There is that underlying Oneness and love that can be shared with anybody when we are in contact with the deeper Self. We distinguish the differences in people and what they bring to the encounter with us, while at the same time sharing this very basic opening to essence. This is truly gratifying.

A teacher is a doorway into the deeper Self, inspiring and guiding others by helping them to turn their attention within and by giving effective methods of moving through the chakra system and beyond. Just as the psychic system with the chakras is a doorway into the deeper state in us, so is a teacher. That does not mean that we should park ourselves next to or in this doorway. It is not useful to just decorate it and admire it, or to try to become like it. The doorway is there to go through, not to just worship and get stuck in front of.

Real gratitude and love for a teacher are shown by taking the responsibility of using the connection as a doorway into our deeper Self. I'm very grateful to my teacher Rudi, but I have never worshipped his form or tried to be like him in any superficial way. That was something he strongly warned against and he did not invite anyone to strive for that. He was unique and accepted that so is everyone else. He was certainly different than I am. He had a different style and personality. I did not necessarily like everything about him or agree with him about everything, but I loved him dearly for the essence that he always invited me and everyone around him to share in. I was and am infinitely grateful for the opportunity to awaken to and share in that essence.

Inscrutable

There is no use going into a serious relationship with a teacher with a focus on the teacher as a person caught in patterns and limitations. This can only lead to conflict and disappointment, and the whole growth process can end before it gets started. We do not necessarily need to like or agree with everything the teacher says and does. We do not even have to like the teacher as a person. The important thing the person shares is not the personal, but the energy at the core which is transpersonal. A teacher's main role is to give spiritual nourishment. For the connection to serve this purpose, a one-pointed focus on taking in that nourishment and digesting it is most important.

Is it necessary to like everything about a cow in order to benefit from its milk? This is a practical question. To get inner nourishment necessitates a deep focus on what the teacher essentially represents: the fundamental creative energy of the Self. It is this energy, and not superficial things, that is the real value we can receive through the connection.

Practicing in connection with a teacher, it is essential at all times to distinguish between what is important and what is not. Having a spiritual teacher does not mean giving up responsibility for our life choices, actions and growth process. No particular lifestyle or rules are demanded by an authentic teacher. What is important is that the teacher's energy field is available to the practitioner and that he or she is open and uses the contact with love and respect. It is only in such an atmosphere that it is possible to receive and digest what unfolds through the relationship. As practitioners, we let ourselves be inspired and filled by spiritual nourishment so that life choices are made in an uplifted and open state, and therefore from a greatly expanded perspective. We surrender to a state in which, as far as possible, ego and identity borders are dissolved and the qualities of the Self are allowed to shine forth.

A person who is capable of serving people in their quest for freedom from the web of karma is a great gift of life, especially to people who deeply seek that freedom. With such a person's wholehearted nurturing and guidance, we can free ourselves from insecurity, self-rejection, guilt, defensiveness, and other negative patterns. Through contact with such a person owe can experience unconditional joy. We can learn to be quiet and centered enough to exist in a simple state marked by love and unlimited pure awareness. We can learn to be grateful for every moment of life, and for life itself.

The liberated state we seek through contact with a spiritual teacher represents a dimension other than the usual attachment to external and secondary circumstances of body and identity. This deeper dimension begins to reveal itself when we let go of clinging to that which is limited by physical, mental, and emotional patterns. This demands moving into something totally unknown, something we are not used to. This is something most people do not know how to do. It is akin to something as common as learning to drive a car. Most people know nothing, or very little, about the car's mechanism. It is a mystery. Still, most people can learn how to make the mechanism function. They learn by observing someone who masters the art of driving, and by experimenting under the guidance of such a person. Trusting the instructor is important, and then following up with experimentation until mastery is gained. We do not have to do much with the mechanism itself, just give it some fuel and learn some simple methods. By repeating the same movements again and again, and by paying attention to the results of these movements, we gradually gain competence and trust in our driving ability.

In the same way that a driving instructor is useful, and in most cases necessary in learning to drive, it is useful, and in the vast majority of cases necessary, to have a competent mentor if we want to be an accomplished musician, artist, scientist, etc. In the work of exploring our being and psychic mechanism and becoming liberated from limitations and patterns, the nourishment and guidance of a competent and trustworthy mentor is even more important. This is so because it is by far the most challenging process a human being can engage in.

Perfect Friendship

Many people expect a teacher to be perfect, whatever that means. This is not possible. No human being is perfect as long as he or she still has a human body and personality. Rudi answered a question about this subject in this way, not long before he passed away:

Have you ever met a perfect guru? Do you know someone who is? The only perfect guru is God, and if you really immerse yourself in God you will continue to grow. I am not trying to replace God for you or anyone else. You take from me because you still do not have the capacity to function. Real spirituality comes after you let go of all teachers so that you have the ability to go directly to God. Then, if you grow that much, you can be a friend.

Letting go of the teacher means that we have grown and ripened to the point where it is no longer necessary to depend on the teacher to help dissolve our tensions for us. We can do it for ourselves; we know how to stay in contact with the fundamental life force without the direct and continuous help of the teacher. We have internalized that contact and support. At that point, it becomes a two-way liberated relationship, Oneness in being where the Self unfolds naturally. This represents the deepest friendship possible in this life, a friendship filled with unconditional love, free energy flow, and mutual respect.

This is the natural process whereby a fruit ripens on the teacher's tree, falling off and growing up to be another functioning and growing tree. Whether that tree is smaller, equal to, or larger than the teacher, whether it has the same color, flower, and fruit is not relevant. The liberation and natural unfolding is what matters. If a teacher chooses to cling to students as fruits on his or her own tree, that clinging creates an unnatural and unhealthy phenomenon, and the original tree will begin to decay. An authentic teacher never needs to control students or hold them back from their natural ripening and separation. About this, Rudi said simply, based on his own experience: *"The most important thing in inner growth is finding a teacher. The second most important thing is to know when to leave that teacher."*

Transmission

Immersed in the Self, the teacher *transmits* spiritual nourishment in the form of the fundamental energy. This is one way of describing it, but what actually happens is that the teacher's inner state has a subtle yet strong effect on the student's inner state. This effect is only possible to the degree the student is open to it. The student's experience of the fundamental energy is awakened in his or her awareness through the contact. As mentioned in chapter one, this process, which is called *shaktipat* (descent of grace), melts inner crystallization.

To the extent that we give ourselves to the contact and inner work, a deep transformation is initiated and starts unfolding. Existential anxiety becomes inner work and expanded creativity. Liberation happens. Through contact with the teacher, the Self becomes tangible. The unknown becomes known. The universal becomes personal. To the extent that we continue surrendering into this state with genuine earnestness, it becomes more real and important than our physical, mental, and emotional aspects.

In relation to a teacher, we need not feel or be controlled or seduced. It is a matter of total contact, not contract. No specific social laws, rules, or patterns must be followed in order for this relationship to result in inner growth and liberation. All we need to do is open ourselves completely to the deepest inner state of another being, and to explore and become established in that state within ourselves. This is done entirely for the sake of our own growth, which, by extension, also truly benefits others. There is no need to feel chained to any particular outer relationship with the teacher. It is the inner connection that counts.

An authentic teacher is a powerful vibration, a ray of light emanating directly from the Self. This vibration warms and uplifts all who let it affect them deeply. In this way, the teacher is like a tuning fork that we can use to tune our own inner vibration or frequency. From non-manifest potential (Shiva), the fundamental energy flows through the teacher and out into the atmosphere. When we open deeply to this most subtle vibration, it touches the deepest dimension within. We sense the vibration in the eyes of the teacher, and in his or her whole being. Then we begin to sense it in our chakra system, and the basic creative energy awakens in our awareness.

In working with a teacher, it is not unusual to experience the first period as a kind of honeymoon. If we are intensely focused on the inner work and the contact, we usually get considerable attention from the teacher. This causes the fundamental energy to awaken so that we begin to catch glimpses of a liberated inner state, and there are often clear and strong transformational experiences during this period. Tensions and patterns begin to dissolve, and then new and deeper tensions and patterns begin to show themselves. Everything buried in the past gradually comes to the surface of conscious attention, showing itself in some form or other, in order to challenge and test the emerging state of liberation glimpsed and that we seek to immerse ourselves in. Every time this happens, it is an opportunity for deeper work and transformation, and for a gradual immersion in the liberated state. This process, which demands letting go of ever deeper layers of tension and patterns as they appear, represents a kind of death-and-rebirth process that has been set in motion, and the process can take a very long time to complete itself.

After the initial honeymoon period, which can vary greatly in length, it is common to come to a point demanding even deeper conscious choice, surrender, and transformation. This occurs naturally in many cases through the practice and contact, without anything dramatic having to be said or done. In other cases, if a practitioner is totally unconscious of some deeper layers of tension and blocks that reveal themselves to the teacher, it may be necessary for him or her to make a conscious intervention, through words, actions, or both, that alerts the practitioner to the need to make a deeper commitment to the process and to surrender resistance to it.

5

PRACTICE

Focusing on giving rather than getting is an essential ingredient in the process of freeing ourselves from the web of karma. It is not being a *do-gooder* with an eye to some specific rewards or in order to be thought of as a good person in society. Rather, it is giving for the sake of bringing about a liberating inner transformation process. For that reason, giving is a prominent feature of Rising Energy Practice. The practice demands turning attention 180 degrees away from being stuck in getting, taking, and holding on to things and circumstances. It demands giving of ourselves to transformation in a variety of ways. This giving is necessary in order for genuine inner growth to occur.

Often people come to hear lectures and say they want to learn a meditation practice even though they are mostly interested in getting hold of something that can quickly restore the inner peace and balance they feel they lack, or that can remove specific problems and challenges they are facing. Many appear to have a use-and-throw-away attitude: As long as they get support, attention, and feel a little better, they are satisfied. As soon as it becomes clear that genuine growth requires giving of ourselves in depth in various ways over an extended time period, the whole thing suddenly becomes a lot less interesting. Very few people are willing to practice in depth for a long enough time that deep and lasting transformation can take place. Many spiritual seekers today tend to regard yoga and meditation the same way they think about material consumption, constantly seeking something new, preferably the very latest on the market. For this reason, relatively few people are willing to commit themselves to a long-term process of inner growth.

The belief that shortcuts to inner growth exist is not realistic and can easily become a cul-de-sac. Genuine transformation of awareness requires a willingness to give deeply of ourselves to practice and inner growth, usually over a long period of time. A realistic formula for this is what Rudi called *"depth over time".* Liberation from the web of karma requires giving deeply to the process for as long as it takes. It requires a lot of persistence and perseverance.

For more and more people in modern Western society, it seems increasingly less interesting to use their time and resources to give to something that offers no immediate ego gratification. Inner practice and selfless service in relation to something deeper than physical, emotional, or so-called self-realization needs, is not so usual. Maslow's Hierarchy of Needs (see Sources) rules most people to a large degree, even though they may never have heard of this hierarchy, which was described by the American psychologist in the 1950s. The theory behind the hierarchy is that as the lower levels of physical survival and safety are satisfied; people are no longer controlled or motivated by these most basic needs. There is little doubt that satisfying these fundamental levels contributes to building a foundation for further development and liberation. Still, from a spiritual perspective, the problem is that many people end up stuck in parts of the hierarchy without ever being fully satisfied. They never get enough.

The notion of giving does not fit in so well with the psychological hierarchy most people are ruled by, which places self-realization with a small 's' as the highest goal and level. This, however, has little to do with inner growth, which, by necessity, requires focus on immersion into the Self with capital 'S', the fundamental stillness and energy at the core of being. In order to open to this dimension, giving of ourselves in a variety of selfless ways is a focus that lies deeper (or higher if you wish) than Maslow's hierarchy. When through such focus inner growth genuinely happens, everything else in life falls into place in a natural way, without any need for chasing or clinging. The Self reveals what is appropriate.

To give selflessly in depth over time builds the inner psychic muscles necessary for growth and liberation. The following five ways to give of ourselves can serve as a framework to describe inner practice in general and

Rising Energy Practice specifically:

1. Give time

2. Give attention

3. Give it up

4. Give in

5. Give back

It is a matter of giving to the Self, to the fundamental stillness and energy of life. These ways of giving create an inner state that benefits not only ourselves, but also everyone we come in contact with, as well as the surrounding environment. To live in deeper contact with the Self means to be filled with a deeper joy, peace, strength, compassion, and power to act. Our range of choice becomes powerfully opened and expanded through contact with the unlimited dimension at the core of being. We have more capacity to give what is really needed by others: genuine attention and compassion, peace, strength, and support. All human beings are essentially one in the sense that each is a manifestation of the fundamental energy. To do something with the intention of harming others, therefore, is to harm ourselves.

Give Time

The most basic way of giving of ourselves is very simply to allow enough time to focus on this task. Those who take their contact with a tradition and practice seriously most often come to this contact and practice with many patterns of thought, reactions, and behavior that need to be released and transformed. Usually they have a sense that they need some kind of change in their inner state and quality of life.

The first thing required for this change to take place is giving ourselves time to practice regularly. It is necessary to consciously turn inward and prioritize the practice highly enough to get seated in meditation at least once a day for at least twenty minutes. It requires prioritizing the maintenance of contact with a teacher highly enough over a long enough time for real changes to happen.

Giving time also means sincerely asking for spiritual growth with all our heart and soul, both in meditation and in daily life. This wish must vibrate throughout our whole energy system. The mantra, "I wish to grow," can be repeated internally until it really feels that this is the most important thing in life. This wish heats up the inner system, melts tension, and allows the energy to flow. We can become aware of a totally different inner state than what we are ordinarily used to. By returning to this wish again and again, contact with that state deeper can be maintained and deepened.

The degree to which inner practice is prioritized determines to a great extent the degree to which liberation from the web of karma is realized. It is a question of continuous commitment, self-discipline and focus. Giving time within whatever daily routines we have is the first requirement.

A classical example of this commitment is the well-known story of Prince Siddhartha Gautama who, more than five hundred years before Christ, became the living Buddha. Until his twenty-ninth year, the prince had lived a very sheltered existence within the walls of his father's palace. He had no experience with suffering, only with the pleasures available within a limited and protected environment. When at last he stepped outside the palace walls and saw the old age, sickness, and suffering there, he became deeply affected and made a promise within not to give up until he reached enlightenment, meaning that he would be liberated from the effects of the suffering he observed through a deeper experience and understanding.

The prince left the palace and the comfortable and protected life he had known there and wandered around India for six years. He practiced yoga and various spiritual techniques of self-sacrifice. Becoming a radical practitioner of renunciation, he rejected all pleasures of life, including that of eating anything more than the bare minimum required for survival. Seeing that this approach did not bring the desired liberation, he at last sat down under the famous Bodhi tree with a total commitment not to move until he had reached his goal. In the process, sitting in total stillness and silence, with all his attention turned inward, he experienced all of his patterns, fears, and temptations in the form of visions. He sat and just observed and surrendered through all that, and in the process he was totally transformed.

Rudi was also a great model of total commitment. Every single day that I was able to observe him directly, it was very clear that everything he thought, felt, and did sprang from his deep wish for inner growth and immersion in the Self. That was the unquestioned first priority in his life. No matter what was happening on any particular day, he found the time for his inner practice. To illustrate the depth of commitment he felt, he mentioned that he had had a vision of himself as a water buffalo, tied to a primitive flour mill. He realized that his life consisted of going around and around inside himself, using his breath and conscious attention like a tireless buffalo, regardless of what was happening in his life. In this way, he was able to grind up tensions, blocks, and patterns within himself. It was a form of selfless service. The result was an abundance of spiritual nourishment and growth for him and others. That is precisely what can happen as we circulate the energy in the chakra system, down the front and up the back. In choosing spiritual growth as our highest priority, everything becomes ground into energy within us, and things in life fall into their natural place.

Inner growth requires giving time to practice regularly throughout the whole transformation process, regardless of how challenging it can be at times. It demands discipline and depth, most often over a whole life time. Without that, the inner muscle system cannot develop to the point that immersion and liberation are possible. If we stop as soon as it becomes a little challenging, or even very difficult, it becomes like opening the door a little bit without stepping inside so that the whole room can be explored. The effect of what has been achieved through disciplined work is, at least to some extent, lost, and it becomes necessary to start over again and again, the whole time just pushing the door open enough to get the same small glimpse each time.

This is no different that learning to master any sport, art or musical instrument in depth. To be a master violinist, for example, requires endless repetition of the same movements over and over again until it becomes a knowledge that sits in the muscles of the fingers and can be performed without much engagement of the rational mind. It demands a tremendous discipline and a very deep commitment. If a violin student stops practicing for a certain period, this bodily knowledge begins to be lost, and the student, even though he or she has entered a very high level before, is prevented from maintaining a level where improvisation and real creative performance can be achieved.

To give ourselves time to practice, it is usually necessary to rearrange priorities and to downgrade certain things we previously invested time and energy in without getting anything of substance in return, seen from an inner growth perspective. Anyone who has a serious interest in such growth eventually faces the need to discern between what gives inner nourishment and what takes time and energy without contributing to growth. Based on this discerning, we need to be willing to consciously change life patterns in order to maximize inner nourishment.

Giving time is important not only in Rising Energy Practice, but also in other types of meditative inner work. All traditions have their practice methods. In Rising Energy Practice, Open Eyes Meditation is a central element. In order to maximize the effect of this practice, it is important to participate with regularity in these events. In addition, it is important to give time to have a regular home practice. To do so, a place can be prepared at home that is quiet, clean, and orderly, with candlelight, incense, pictures, and things that support the practice.

Give Attention

Anytime we sit down to meditate, it is necessary to turn the attention from the external world to the world within. This is done by consciously focusing attention on the inner wish to grow, on the breath, the chakra system, and on the presence of the infinite dynamic stillness at the core of being. This conscious focusing is away from thoughts. Still, thoughts will appear and demand attention even as the focus is turned within. The way to handle that is not to reject or struggle with the thoughts, but simply allow them to recede into the background, like clouds in the sky. As the ability to hold attention inside gradually improves, thoughts become less and less a distraction. They become more and more insubstantial in the sky of our wide open witness awareness.

Bhagavan Nityananda, a well-known Indian yogi and saint who died in 1961, sat in his later years mostly immersed in the basic energy of life. He did not speak much, but he did say this about turning the attention within: "Return to the Self within and know your own secret. The universe is inside you and you are inside the universe. The inner Self is the One dancing in all—the One who is here and the One who is there."6

Breath is a very important movement to pay attention to in inner practice. Through it, one begins to make conscious contact with the Self, the quiet, pulsating core of existence Nityananda called the *"sky of the heart"*. In practice, it is important to sit in a comfortable position while remaining as fully alert as possible. Eyes should be closed, the sitting posture comfortable, either in a traditional cross-legged posture or on a chair. Hands should rest on the thighs, palms up, with the thumbs and index fingers meeting and making a circle. The head is tilted slightly upward to open the throat and chest, and the belly is relaxed so that it moves freely with the incoming and outgoing breath. It is by becoming aware of the breath and the subtle still- points within it as it turns from inward to outward and outward to inward, that we establish ourselves in the present moment.

The incoming breath is done while bringing the attention from the top of the head to the base of the spine. Then there is a still-point to notice at the base of the spine between the in-breath and the out-breath. With the outgoing breath the attention is brought from the base of the spine to the top of the head. There the still-point is noticed while briefly holding the breath before the next in-breath is taken. It is a deep, slightly slowed breath in four phases, done with full inner attention. It is a conscious breath keeping attention away from thoughts and instead connecting with the

or an open wound. Anger and fear cause the stomach area to tighten. At other times, the heart suddenly opens in a kind of boundless joy. We feel grateful to be alive, or we may feel safe and strong in the situation we are in, and breathe deeply and calmly into the stomach.

The state of the chakras is closely connected with and has a deep effect on our thoughts, reactions, and actions, and vice versa. Changes occur in these centers in response to everything we feel, think, say, and do. In turn, what we think, feel, say, and do have an effect on the centers. Our chakras are like doorways into the core of being, into the universal dimension beyond time and space. In order to explore this subtle dimension within, giving attention to the chakras allows a process of cleaning them so that they can open as doorways for attention to move into a deeper state of awareness.

The chakras are openings into the deeper state which is free of ego. In that deeper awareness, the ego does not catch our attention. We open and allow the desires and patterns of ego to flow within the chakra system as creative energy. We open completely to the deeper Self and allow it to be in control. In contact with this deeper state, everything becomes much more natural. Things happen spontaneously and often surprisingly. *"How did I end up here? How did I get to this?"* Life becomes much more of an adventure. We become more like a child in some ways. Without losing our intelligence we become able to relax and enjoy our circumstances more, and our circumstances can spontaneously change. We have more wisdom and compassion. We become more playful and creative. It is exciting and uplifting, and it is very practical.

Life is an opportunity to realize who we are and to anchor ourselves in that realization. This helps us deal with our life more gratefully and compassionately. It is a powerful transformation process, and it can be quite challenging. As we work inside ourselves to let go of attachment to layers of our identity, we move into a void which can be experienced as a wonderful place to be, totally free of problems, or as a place full of uncertainty and anxiety. This void is called the *turya* state. Entering it can be liberating, but it can also bring about anxiety because it is a state demanding that we open to the unknown. If we are very attached to being in control, it is uncomfortable at first to face the need to let go of control.

If we want the transformation, we have to tolerate the process of opening to the reality that at the core we are nothing but pure potential and energy. In opening to that we discover that we are essentially nothing but an open state, one with everything. We surrender the small stuff. Compared with the deeper awareness of the Self, everything is more or less small stuff. From the perspective of our center, all our attachments in the outer rim of life are relatively unimportant. We think they are more important than they really are because they belong to the person we have been conditioned to think we are. We have been trained to think that various aspects of our identity are indispensible, that we must hold on to them at all costs, in all circumstances.

It is necessary to develop an identity that allows us to function in society. There is nothing wrong with that. Unfortunately, though, our identity tends to become a prison, blocking our deeper awareness. If we are not able to go deeper and recognize that our identity is a secondary reality, basically an emanation of the primary reality of the Self, it becomes a web that catches us rather than a manifestation that shines on us as the reflected light of the Self.

The flow of energy in the chakra system is extremely subtle, and it may take some time before anything other than blockage and tensions are experienced there. That needs not be discouraging. It is as a melting process that starts slowly but intensifies with time. It is like looking for something barely visible, like listening for soft, subtle sounds, or feeling for a profoundly gentle touch or barely discernible movement. We use all our inward sensitivity to open to the subtle dimension within us. The inner work is to become conscious of the mechanism, to become quiet and focused enough to experience the flow there, and the dynamic stillness that is its source.

Give It Up

The inner wish and focus on the breath, chakras, and flow, preferably in conjunction with contact with a qualified teacher, cause the fundamental energy to awaken in our awareness, bringing with it glimpses of liberation. The web of karma has no affect in the moments when we are in that state. At the same time, as a direct result of our work and such glimpses, the tension that is frozen within as blocks and patterns begins to make itself known, so that that we can face it and allow it to dissolve. In other words, as glimpses into a deeper state occur, so do glimpses of our own human limitations in the form of attachment to tension and patterns.

The veiling force, i.e. the web of karma, presents more powerful tests than ever at this stage. Disturbances, conflicts, and challenges tend to appear. These challenges test the seriousness of our wish, our ability to continue the inner work, and to hold to and deepen awareness of the state that has been briefly encountered. All this can be faced and transcended by consciously letting go, by giving up attachment in the form of chasing and clinging in these various test situations.

As we deepen our practice, focusing attention within and letting go of chasing and clinging to patterns and identity, it is not uncommon to become aware of a certain inner emptiness. This is a good thing because it represents the openness that we need to become familiar and comfortable with in order to grow inside. This empty feeling is a reaction to the void mentioned above, and it can be uncomfortable, frightening, or even boring.

We are not used to this void, and the tendency is to want to escape as quickly as possible from the discomfort of it by going back to something we are familiar with, such as self-pity, complaints against others, anger, criticism or even mental, emotional and physical attacks on others. If we allow the emptiness we feel to fill up with such thoughts, emotional reactions, and actions, this is precisely what keeps us from experiencing the deeper reality of the void. The void is not really empty at all but rather full of vibrating potential, something called *spanda* in the literature of Kashmir Shaivism. Giving up attachment to habitual thoughts, reactions, and actions is particularly important in the process of opening to the void.

To give up on chasing and clinging is a key to inner growth. It is necessary to surrender attachment to specific tensions, blocks and patterns as they come up. This is done by shifting attention from these attachments into the power within which is vastly greater than the limited ego elements. Even though we may use a teacher, tradition, and philosophy as inspiration to give up attachment to specific ego elements, it is not the teacher, tradition, or philosophy we surrender to. What we are letting go into is the deepest core of being, that which is universal and boundless. By surrendering to this dimension, and thus gaining experiential contact with it, we rise above that which previously seemed so frightening, meaningless, or negative.

Through surrender to the infinite, things that before seemed like huge, insurmountable problems and obstacles suddenly become small details we can include and live with. Certain aspects of life may still be difficult and challenging, but they are no longer too big to rise above. They may even begin to seem interesting as we discover how much can be learned from challenges and how nourishing it can be to respond positively to them. It can release a tremendous amount of energy flow and change of awareness. Apparent gigantic boulders that before were blocking our path now become the very stepping stones under our feet as we walk that path.

The more we practice the more we can enter into pure awareness at will. It starts by having some glimpses of it, and is followed by having longer periods of immersion in it. Finally we end up having the ability to open the door and enter that awareness no matter what situation we are in, even if it is in an unpleasant situation dominated by ego identity and even conflict. We may be in a meeting with many big egos involved, and our own ego might react strongly to what goes on. There may be a lot of tension in the situation. In the middle of our reaction to it, we can pull our attention back and not allow ourselves to be so involved that we get sucked in and seriously disturbed. We can go deeply within ourselves into a more open, non-attached state. We can realize the degree to which expression of attachment to opinions and desires is a kind of play. We see that the world of ego attachment is really limited and can be quite crazy. In it, people are so conditioned to react in accordance with the fight or flight syndrome that no deeper awareness is possible. People go on automatic and suddenly they are caught in some reaction, opinion or irresolvable conflict.

We may think about things we do not like as negative or meaningless. This very labeling reveals that we are caught in certain mental, emotional, and behavioral patterns. It means we have something specific to let go of. It means we have to open up more and expand within so that we can embrace and digest not only what we like but also what we find repugnant. Through practice, we gain the non-attachment that frees us from the need to mentally or emotionally judge anything as negative or meaningless. In a more open and liberated inner state, we move forward in life while simply digesting everything we meet in the grand inner and outer landscape. We appreciate all the details of these landscapes without judgment.

To give up control is to open up to reality as it is, without repressing or denying anything. That requires trust and letting go of attachment to thoughts and emotional reactions. Instead, we allow the fundamental energy to dominate our awareness and show us the way. Then we are no longer stuck in what we like or dislike. The energy within these elements is set free and what we experience is simply energy movements in the deeper awareness.

To really grow inside, life must be digested whole, with all its joys, difficulties, and sorrows. Instead of repressing, denying, or running away from pain or difficulty, we open to it, allow it to dissolve into energy flow in the chakra system; we circulate it within. This makes it nourishment for transformation. We digest it and grow inside from it. This digesting happens best if we eat slowly and take the time to process what we eat very well before we eat again. It requires time, deep relaxation and awareness. The process of digesting inner nourishment is no different than the process of keeping a baby well fed. If we stuff more food into the baby's mouth than it can swallow, food will be rejected and spat out. It is necessary to give the baby enough time to digest the food already given before feeding it again, even if the baby cries for more because it tastes good.

Inner growth demands a continuous expansion of what we are capable of taking in and digesting. In order for such expansion to take place, we consciously and deeply open up inside. To the extent that we struggle to grasp life's events and circumstances through rational analysis and in order to feel in control, we are simply wasting our time and energy. If we let go of these patterns, limitations, and the need to know anything at all with certainty in the analytical mind, then a totally different level of inner experience and wisdom emerges and is made available to us.

Give In

The giving up of attachment to specific thoughts and reactions, and the giving in to full awareness of the Self, are two sides of the same thing. We have to give up attachment to specifics in order to give in to the deeper underlying reality. Both are forms of surrender. It is only by letting go of specific attachments as we become aware of them that immersion into a simple, open inner state without boundaries becomes a genuine possibility. Letting go of specific attachments allows the Self to assert itself more in our awareness. Another way to say that is that a very strong pull begins to assert itself from this dimension, inviting us to give in to its deeper joy, freedom and energy. In giving in to this pull towards a deeper state of awareness again and again, we gradually become more familiar with it and feel safe in taking more regular refuge there.

While the dynamic stillness of that boundless state may be very frightening when first encountered, an unbelievable inner strength, joy, and freedom is gained as we get used to living in contact with that state. To live no longer dependent upon and limited by the security of comfortable and familiar patterns means giving in to the mystery of the unknown. A deep inner transformation is set in motion as soon as we have the courage to enter into that dimension, and it is reinforced by every entry thereafter. This is, of course, much easier said than done. It requires continuous deep practice and transformation. In this process, guidance of a teacher can be very helpful.

To give in to the deepest state is to surrender into unconditional love, to open to life just as it is, to the practice, to teacher, to family, friends, work, etc., without chasing after or clinging to any of it. We become anchored in unconditional love without needing to know the details of where it will lead. We simply love the mystery and wonder of life, and the joy and energy at its core. To give in to the Self is to love the fundamental energy of life without clinging to the effects of it. Surrender leads to a rich, amazing experience full of surprises and challenges. It is surfing on the ocean of awareness which can be both exhilarating and scary. When we manage to ride the natural waves of this ocean, we feel the power of mastery vibrating throughout our entire being. We become one with the ocean and its movements.

Ego related experience is limited, familiar, and safe. Experience of the fundamental life force is marked by freedom, joy, and a clear focus on the here and now. Still, the fundamental life force can be frightening in its boundlessness, power, and fullness. As in surfing, in order to ride the waves, fear must be overcome and transformed.

In the experience of and immersion in the fundamental life force, we become liberated from the burdens and limitations of a chasing and clinging approach to life. We are freed from the tyranny of mental, emotional, and behavioral patterns and are filled with spontaneous creativity and gratitude for just being able to breathe and be. By fully giving in to the power of deeper awareness, the recognition fully dawns on us at last: *"I really am the Self. I am not a thing but a boundless unfolding process"*. We recognize that in this process all tension and limited patterns are transformed into an experience of simple, pulsating awareness. This happens by shifting attention away from focus on tension and patterns and by letting go into the core of being.

*

A method of fully giving in to the Self is found in the tantric text Vijnanabhairava (Divine Consciousness).8 It is the simple practice (dharana) of tuning into the om sound, the high pitched electrical sound vibrating in space. We can sense the vibration at the top of our head, in the crown chakra, and we can consciously bring it into our whole being. In order to hear or sense it we have to get really quiet first. We have to center ourselves in a wide open, non-attached state.

Awareness of the Self requires not being stuck in any thought constructs. We cannot be thinking about everything under the sun. Of course thoughts will come automatically, but following them and being attached to them does not work. Rather, we let them flow naturally in the background, in a wide open state. We gently observe the thoughts as emerging and dissolving within the open awareness. Then the thoughts are not experienced as ego but rather as an aspect of the natural flow of creative energy within the Self.

Being aware of this extremely subtle vibration requires being centered and connected with the silence at our core. When we get in touch with that silence we can sense the very subtle *om* sound coming in at the top of the head. It is the fundamental universal vibration. If we tune into that and allow it to flow into us, we are flooded with healing energy and become immersed in the universal dimension. To the extent that we do it long enough and deeply enough, it is highly purifying and transformative.

We can draw the om sound into ourselves while we circulate the attention within using the breathing as described earlier. We repeat the *So Hum (I am That-That I am)* mantra, so on the in-breath, hum on the out-breath. We follow the breath down the front to the base of the spine on the in-breath while saying *so* inside, and then up to the top of the head while saying *hum* inside. We become aware that between the inhalation and the exhalation, and also between the exhalation and inhalation, there are still-points, as described earlier. We allow attention to expand into these still-points, feeling them open into a boundless space. The mantra and the om sound fill awareness and the still-points expand, taking the place of thoughts. Full attention on the om sound, the mantra and the opening into unlimited space dissolves attachment to thinking and sensory experience.

Another text that describes how to open into universal awareness is Pratyabhijnavrdiam (Secret of Recognition). It deals with absolute truth and how we can recognize it. It clarifies that this absolute nature is not dependent on any judgment, focus, language or action. It is free of all conceptualization and thinking, only emerging in our awareness when we open fully in non-attachment.

As long as we live in the world and have a body and identity, it is always a matter of moving in and out of the state of pure awareness. When we are not in it, then ego becomes more predominant, and that is fine and necessary. Ego patterns are needed to function in the world. But gradually we can become skilled at moving into this space of consciousness and energy that we *are* at a deeper level, while we are going through whatever we are going through on a physical, mental, and emotional level.

Another tantric method (dharana) described in the Vijnanabhairava is to use any kind of strong emotion or desire as a starting point for beginning to recognize fundamental energy and pure awareness. Using the method, we just observe the emotion or desire and follow it to its source without getting caught in it and without worrying. We refrain from allowing the mind to react with mental analysis: *"What is this feeling, and what should I do?"* The more the mind is engaged in analysis of emotion, and the more it tries to control it, the more mental suffering is produced. By circulating the energy of the emotion inside, that energy rises to the top of the head and produces more freedom, wisdom and compassion.

*

A mistake is not necessarily something negative. With the right inner attitude, we can see something in useful in what the mind might call negative. Anything can be a learning experience. To be in a non-attached state and to move with the awareness that there is a deeper state free of worries that can be drawn from allows us to no longer have to be victims of our ego. It is simple and practical. Our ego is functioning, but we can be in that deeper state while we are allowing the ego to do its thing. Instead of being caught on automatic, allowing negative karmic things to play out and create more tension and complexity, we can have some non-attachment and humor in relation to ego. We can say to ourselves: *"Well, here I go again, reacting according to one of my old patterns".* We can chuckle and be happy that we can go through that realization into a deeper level of awareness.

When we gain the ability to be in the ego while at the same time seeing it for what it is, then we can also let go of it. It is like the fierce tiger that is revealed to be just a paper tiger. It is no longer frightening. It is not dangerous. Whether what we see is our tendency to judge by blaming everybody else or by blaming ourselves, we do not get stuck in it. There is no longer any need for guilt, fear or doubt. Ego is no longer threatening. We can let it be and flow while enjoying the energy and awareness at its core. The Rising Energy Practice is useful in transcending and dissolving ego issues in everyday life. The tantric texts say that if we do at least one of the methods (dharanas) described in them regularly every day and maintain some awareness of it, we will transform and eventually be free of all attachment to ego patterns and tendencies. We will recognize the energy and pure awareness at the core of being and become one with that.

Give Back

Giving back involves a conscious extension of the experience of the fundamental energy, or flow, from inside us to the outer dynamics of our life, to the daily routines of life such as work, family, society, and the environment. It means being aware of the exchange, the flow, between the inner and the outer aspects of our life. We consciously work to create a flow between what we experience within during meditation and what we experience in everyday life, expanding the inner experience to include all our activities and relationships. In this way, the creative capacity of the fundamental energy is allowed to fully unfold and express itself. As meditation practice becomes integrated with life in the world, we discover that the fundamental energy really is a limitless resource. By extending the energy into the outer dynamics of our life, we gradually become more expanded, more liberated human beings.

The fundamental energy is the same as unconditional love. It gives of itself without limitation; it is the basic power of the universe. It is never diminished by being given away. It has the capacity to boundlessly unfold from within itself, and to give of itself without limits. To unify with that force requires a totally open attitude. Anything else creates limitation and conflict.

We give back to that which supports us and gives us inner nourishment by serving it without any expectations of a specific outcome or ego satisfaction. In Sanskrit this is called *seva* which means selfless service. This is a common component of practice within ashrams in India and other Eastern cultures.

In the course of everyday life outside an ashram structure there are also unlimited opportunities for selfless service. It can be as simple as bringing a co-worker, boss or employee a cup of coffee because we know the person loves it and because the time is right for it. By consciously being open to the person, and to the general flow of energy in the workplace, we can sense that such a simple gesture would benefit the person and also the team work and cooperation of the overall situation. Then we just do it without expecting any personal ego reward for it.

The same is possible in family or social life. We can consciously refrain from getting stuck in our own or other people's limitations and instead act from a deeper awareness. This means opening up inside while not reacting with vengeance or self judgment in conflict situations. We can say we are sorry if we have expressed ourselves from being stuck in ego limitation, and we can look for opportunities to express ourselves from deeper awareness. In this way, we can invite other people in our family, social and work life to participate in an exchange less dominated by tension and conflict.

To serve situations in life without being limitted by selfish thinking or attracted to a particular outcome is something that requires training. Selfless service is not a matter of doing things for others out of a sense of duty. Seva means to do things in a state of total openness, as a gesture of love and service to life itself. To accomplish this requires holding on to the deeper wish to grow, prioritizing practice, and letting go of attachment within life situations. Seva begins within, and it happens by being conscious of our own inner state, by letting go of tensions, and by opening our heart, regardless of what others may or may not do. Seva is inherently selfless, yet it is not a repression or denial of who we are. Rather, it is an affirmation of what we may potentially become: the best person we can be. We make deliberate efforts to react to others not with tension but with love and respect. We consciously work to create balance, peace, joy, and harmony in our surroundings. All of this, of course, requires discipline, especially in the beginning.

Life is full of opportunities to give back in this way, regardless of what circumstances we find ourselves in. It may be as simple as being aware that a colleague, family member, or friend has an especially difficult day, and therefore approaching them with extra care and compassion. When we are trapped in egoistical thinking and action, we usually relate to others with a focus on our own self-preservation, meaning that we are ruled by basic survival instincts that bring us into either defensive or attacking reaction. This reaction needs to be transcended. We let go of wanting to control people and situations according to limiting patterns and expectations. Instead, as much as possible, we act and speak from a deeper awareness of Self, in a way that best serves the situation as a whole. Selfless service means giving to others what they truly need, not what we think they ought to need.

Two Wings

A practitioner of what is described here can be likened to a bird that needs balanced and full use of both wings to get off the ground and stay in the air, flying as it needs to. The inner effort of wish, conscious breath and inner attention is one wing, the other is relaxing, surrendering, and letting go. If there is too much effort without enough letting go, a flapping with only one wing occurs, causing the practitioner to end up going around in circles without getting anywhere except around and down. If there is not enough letting go, there is not enough power to keep the practitioner uplifted in all circumstances. Letting go is an inner act, not just a passive avoidance. Both wings need to be strong and active in order to deal with gravity and the shifting winds of life.

In practicing, we can easily notice when one or the other of the two wings is too active while the other is too passive. If we huff and puff excessively with a very strong wish and deep breathing while holding the breath, we tend to become overheated and filled with inner tension. If we want too much, without having the necessary surrender to the deeper Self, dissolution and absorption of the tension and material we are working with cannot happen. The inner state becomes too heavy and pressured for energy to flow and rise. On the other hand, if we don't focus deeply enough on the wish to grow and on the breath and chakras, the material that needs to be surrendered, and thus serve as a kind of fuel for flight, does not become apparent enough in our awareness. We end up without enough material and tension to burn, and rising energy is not possible in the long run. Inner effort and letting go are equally important in the transformation process. Both need to be used as required.

6

TANTRA

The Tantric texts that perhaps best describe the foundation and essence of Rising Energy Practice are found within the tradition of Kashmir Shaivism. This tradition, appeared in the Northwestern part of India during the eighth century and left a detailed written explanation of Tantric philosophy and practice. Although they can be difficult to read and comprehend due to their use of many Indian terms, these texts shed much light on the practice and process described in this book, hopefully in terms that are simpler to understand. Kashmir Shaivism emphasizes inner growth through a process of opening the heart, feeling the flow in the chakra system, surrender, and finding the Self within. It aims to reach the nothingness and everything at the core of life, becoming immersed in the dynamic stillness of Shiva/Shakti awareness.

According to Kashmir Shaivism, dynamic stillness is infinite consciousness with unlimited creative power. Shiva is the consciousness that lies at the core of all energy unfolding and manifestation. In the infinite ocean of consciousness, a basic creative impulse (*spanda*) begins to stir and prepare for movement, like the creative impulse that stirs in an artist before placing the pencil or brush to paper or canvas. From this impulse, vibrations (*Shakti*) unfold, interact with each other, and become more and more complex systems. Dynamic stillness is the fundamental source of all existence. It is infinite awareness with unlimited potential, the foundation of all energy movement and manifestation. It can manifest as anything, anywhere, anytime. It is the essence of being, the ocean of unlimited possibilities. It is the source of our life and contains within itself the power to manifest absolutely anything. Human beings are energy manifestations or waves in that ocean while still identical with it.

The dynamic stillness of *Shiva/Shakti* is the union of the masculine and feminine principles of reality. This is often referred to as *the One, the Absolute, or the Self.* Sometimes it is just called God, or the Divine. At times the male aspect of stillness and consciousness *(Shiva)* is emphasized; at other times the female aspect of creative energy *(Shakti)* is emphasized. The female aspect is sometimes referred to as the Goddess, the ruler of cosmic existence. Using some of these terms in this book is to point to the experience of the fundamental reality and its inherent qualities.

The fundamental power that springs out in the Self is called *Shakti* in its universal form and *Kundalini* in its individual form, as it manifests in human beings. This core power unfolds to become all that is manifest without ever becoming different than or separate from the underlying Consciousness. The symbol of this unfolding is the dancing Shiva. The dance is all manifestation within the infinite ocean of Consciousness, from the subtlest vibration to the most solid physical form. The dance is everything that springs forth from the ocean of Consciousness, including us as human beings, including all our thoughts, feelings, and actions. All that exists, has existed, and will exist springs out of the ocean of Consciousness, without losing the essence of the ocean. A wave is a wave, but it is still essentially the ocean. Likewise, material form and the formless spiritual are two aspects of one reality, a continuous, non-dualistic singularity.

In the Rising Energy Practice, we do not aim to repress, deny, or reject anything as different from the Self. It is a non-dualistic Tantric philosophy and practice, rooted in the principle of Oneness. The aspect of stillness full of potential and the manifest dynamic aspect of creative unfolding are two sides of that Oneness. This can be experienced within. New things become possible as we connect with the stillness and creative energy inside ourselves. The purpose of life is to experience the peaceful openness and powerful energy of that Oneness—not by avoiding things but by embracing them with an attitude of non-attachment, with unconditional love and joy. The point is to embrace and digest everything in life as inner nourishment, not to avoid life in the world by isolating ourselves from it.

This is as relevant today as it was more than a thousand years ago, perhaps even more so, due to the materialism and individualism prevalent in modern society. Earlier meditation masters within the Tantric tradition developed a practice and philosophy designed to explore the deepest reality of life as a human being, and to make it possible for us to awaken and immerse ourselves in that. They discovered that it is possible to live in a state of total freedom and well-being.

Fundamental Life Force

In Kashmir Shaivism and other Tantric traditions the vital fundamental life force on the human level is called Kundalini. Christianity and other traditions also have names for subtle energy flow in the body, such as Holy Spirit and Chi. These words describe something akin to Kundalini, but do not necessarily mean exactly the same. In relation to spiritual growth and liberation, it does not matter what name we give the fundamental power and subtle energy within us. What is important in this context is that we dissolve our tensions, blocks, and patterns so that increased energy flow and creativity can occur.

Experience of the fundamental life force within us can arise through the use of powerful natural or chemical drugs, or during especially strong life situations that provoke an opening to that which lies beneath our superficial, day-to-day life patterns, for example losing a person one is very close to, the breakup of marriage, a life-threatening illness, or traumatic accidents or incidents. Both powerful drugs and life-altering events can temporarily shake a person out of normal, everyday consciousness and cause Kundalini to rise in the person's awareness. However, especially in the case of drugs, this Kundalini experience comes at a very high price, because the psychic system is weakened in the process of taking them.

Developing permanent contact with the fundamental energy is not likely through either drugs or strong life situations. Such causes do not readily allow full digestion of the experience. This is because, in the majority of cases, the inner psychic muscle system is not strong enough to assimilate the experience or master the necessary transformation. These causes as such are therefore just as likely to weaken and entangle us as they are likely to free us and make us stronger through the awakened Kundalini.

The best and surest way to cause the Kundalini to rise in our awareness and learn to master the transformation process required to become immersed in it, is through in-depth inner practice over time, in contact with a teacher. Through such practice and contact, the chakra system is strengthened and opened. What is dissolved in the transformation process is consumed and digested. By consciously allowing blocks, patterns, and tensions to dissolve over time through practice and *shaktipat (descent of Grace)*, Kundalini awareness occurs naturally, and we become strong enough to absorb its effects over time, until we achieve full immersion. In the process, we starve our illusions and feed the deepest reality in us, using the practice and contact.

Even though Rising Energy Practice has its roots in Tantra and therefore in both Hinduism and Buddhism, and despite the fact that it is well expressed by the philosophy of Kashmir Shaivism, it is not correct to say that the practice is a religion. It is not an *"ism"*. There is no official dogma. There are not a lot of rules that define what we can and cannot do; nor are there a lot of concepts we must believe in or not believe in. The focus of this practice is to provide support, nourishment, and guidance to practitioners through certain methods, in order for them to find their own answers regarding what does or does not contribute to their inner growth. As we develop the capacity to discern its voice in our life, the Self provides the answers.

In many different cultures throughout the ages, religion has often been used as a political means of controlling people, not freeing them. This is not the point of genuine inner practice with liberation as the goal. In Rising Energy Practice, the goal is inner growth for anyone who wants it. The philosophical concepts you believe in, and what name you choose to call what you do, are far less important than the results of the practice and contact you engage in.

Play of Consciousness

Kashmir Shaivism says that the Self is pure Consciousness and presence, an all-encompassing intelligence with the capacity to manifest. Consciousness exists without support or relation to anything else; it just *is*, has always been, and will always be. At the same time, it is free to unfold from within itself and become everything, without ever losing its essence. Our individual being, comprised of all its thoughts, feelings and actions, is never separate from that essence.

This understanding of Oneness, which was discovered, explored, and described by practicing yogis more than a thousand years ago, is now being confirmed by modern science. In his book *Revolution in Science* referred to earlier, Ervin Laszlo points out that research in several fields of modern science—physics, cosmology, biology, and consciousness—confirms the ancient Eastern worldview of a unified underlying reality. He asserts that the essence of the new scientific view is that *"the universe as a whole is a coherent and interactive cosmic field."* This is called the *psi-field* or *akasha-field* in modern science, and it is identical with the Self (Shiva/Shakti) as described in Kashmir Shaivism. In the preface of his book, Laszlo writes:

[T]he subtle ocean of fluctuating energies which is the source of galaxies, stars and planets, as well as life and thought on the Earth and possibly on other planets in the entire cosmic space. . . . The psi-field is not only the original source of everything that appears in space and time, but also nature's constant and continual memory. It is a warehouse of everything that for all times has happened in the universe, and it is the subtle and always present information bank for all that ever will take place.9

Five Acts of Consciousness

In alignment with this modern scientific view, Kashmir Shaivism describes the three major acts or powers of Consciousness as creation, maintenance, and dissolution. In addition, it presents two more acts or powers: the power to conceal and the power to reveal.

Creation is the Self's power to manifest whatever it wants, whenever it wants, wherever it wants. Maintenance is the Self's power to hold the creation moving within certain time frames. Dissolution is the Self's power to absorb back into itself what has been created and maintained. The two additional acts or powers Kashmir Shaivism points to are: concealing (veiling) and revealing. Veiling is the ability of the Self to conceal its essential nature from its own creation (*samsara*). This includes the creation of the web of karma. Revealing, or revelation, is the power to remove the veiling and thereby dissolve the web of karma so the true essence (*moksha*) becomes available in our human awareness. In revelation, the underlying pure Consciousness is recognizable to human beings.

It is our ego limitations that cause us to be unaware of the natural unity at the core of our existence, the dynamic stillness that is the ground of all of life's cycles. Usually, we get stuck in the dynamics and effects that unfold within that ground, especially in the dissolution phase, for example when a pattern or relationship is coming to an end. We prefer to hold on to what is, and we have a tendency to become mired in thoughts and reactions in relation to what is happening. This becomes increased tension and suffering. We do not have the holistic perspective that allows for change as something that is totally natural and actually beneficial. We may understand that dissolution and death are necessary in nature and in the universe in order for new things to be born, but it is much easier to accept and surrender to this universal reality than on the level of our own personal life. It is exactly for this reason that it is important to have contact with a guide who can be a living example of this possibility, and who can support us through difficult times until we learn to master our inner state through the death-and-rebirth process.

Just as dissolution is a natural phase on earth and in the whole universe, so it is in the process of inner development. In fact, dissolution is the only thing that can lead to liberation from ego limitations and bring about deeper and broader experiences in life. Rather than fighting against this natural process and repressing or denying the pain we experience, it is beneficial, in these periods, to consciously let go and keep our focus on inner growth. By taking one small step at a time, slowly but surely digesting the pain involved, we can discover the sweetness and wisdom at the core of the pain. By being alert to where we are in a cycle, and not forgetting the deeper wish to grow, we can, over time, learn to trust that after dissolution new creativity always follows, and new experiences and possibilities will appear in our life. The important thing is to allow the doors that are closing to do so, without unnecessary mental and emotional drama, even though the situation may seem unjust or beyond our limited understanding and individual perspective. To the extent that we manage to do this, we are ready to walk through new doors in a natural way as they begin to open.

Usually people are so attracted to and ensnared by superficial effects that they do not recognize and immerse themselves in their source, the dynamic stillness they actually are. Experience of that reality is, for the most part, veiled from awareness. Tantra, including the Rising Energy Practice, invites the dissolution of that veiling force by allowing the force of revelation to be the center of attention.

As noted above, the veiling force is the power of the Self to hide its true reality and qualities. It causes us to be caught in a limited understanding and experience of reality. To be caught in this veiling is to not see or experience anything other than the limitations of ego awareness. It is to experience existence as dualistic. This is the illusion of the ego. It sees itself as separate from everything else, and with the separation there is usually a sense of emptiness, conflict, or lack of real meaning. The ego sees itself as separate from others, from nature, and from the whole. In this way, the veiling force binds and blinds us, locking us in a prison of darkness. This is the power of the Self to create tension, blockages, and illusion. Fortunately, the Self also makes liberation possible, through revelation. Working deeply within over a long enough time, the Self removes the obstacles to recognition of its full reality. Conscious work inside is required to dissolve tension and blocks in the chakra system. Surrender to the fundamental energy experience reveals the dynamic stillness hidden at the core of tensions and crystallization.

Why these veiling and liberating forces are a part of the unfolding of the Self is a good question. Liberation sounds good, but why does the Self veil itself, allowing tension, blocks, and suffering? Well, this is just how it is. It is something to be surrendered into. The Tantric tradition answers only by saying that it is *lila*, or the play of consciousness. This is in keeping with the Buddha's teaching that suffering is one of life's universal truths. Kashmir Shaivism says it is the Self's possibility of unfolding and experiencing itself in its full reality. Without veiling and suffering, there would be no experience of release and liberation. The contrast is necessary, as are the two opposite poles of a mutually dependent whole: night and day, high and low, pain and pleasure. Without one, the other could not exist.

Through practice and experience of the flow within, we gradually understand that the value of suffering is that it motivates us to work toward and surrender ourselves into liberation. That possibility is something we can be very grateful for. The alternative is to remain caught in the limiting veiling aspect of the Self and to go endless rounds caught in the web of karma.

In the Pratyabhijnarhdayam, one of Kashmir Shaivism's main texts, you can read that:

. . . if one does not understand the process of the five main powers, one is confused by one's own forces and becomes victim of samsara (veiling). If one can fully understand this whole process by turning the attention to one's deepest inside, then one will rise to the level of the Self and become identical with the fundamental Consciousness.10

For genuine liberation to occur, we learn to live in a state of unconditional gratitude for and surrender to the fundamental Consciousness. We learn to embrace and absorb reality as we meet it, in its entirety, and to open to and digest our own pain. This is recognized as the major purpose of the life we have been given: to open ourselves and reach toward this liberation.

7

ATTITUDE

A classic and inspiring explanation of the inner attitude that allows for freedom from the web of karma is found in the Bhagavad Gita, which means the Song of God.11 This historical poem was written in India many hundreds of years ago and, most likely, originates from the centuries either just before or after the birth of Christ. The poem, which has inspired countless people throughout the ages, perfectly illustrates how the circumstances of life can capture us and make us feel stuck, as well as how we can choose to rise above them and become liberated. Even though the poem is a product of a totally different time and culture than our own, its universal theme remains highly relevant for all human beings, regardless of time and place.

The Bhagavad Gita explains that if we want liberation from karma, we need to take responsibility for doing the work that presents itself naturally and lies right in front of us, without clinging to any particular outcome or chasing after ego satisfaction. We are asked to selflessly serve the deeper Self, and life as a whole, as best we can. In relation to this, it is only our inner attitude and posture that matters, not the outcome. This means that we are responsible for completing what we have attracted or chosen in this life, and that which unfolds naturally. We need to start where we are and love the life we are given, the very life that we find ourselves in here and now. We need to give ourselves over to that, without expectations. Working in this way, we allow more of the fundamental life force and its infinite power to penetrate into our awareness, marking both our inner and outer life with flow and awareness. As this happens, our creativity blossoms and we gain greater capacity to participate in the vitality of life. Any abilities and powers that we may acquire through this process are not for the purpose of consuming or controlling more but simply to serve in a superior way, to give more back to life itself.

In the poem, the prince and warrior Arjuna finds himself on the battlefield in a confrontation between two great armies. He has been betrayed by some of his own kinsmen, who are now confronting him on the other side of the battlefield. He has lost his land and many of his closest relatives and friends. As he faces the decisive battle, Arjuna struggles bitterly with what appears to be an impossible choice: he must either kill his own family members, or fail to fulfill his duty as a prince, warrior, and protector of the loyal people who desperately need his leadership. Either alternative will seriously violate the social order. The dilemma causes Arjuna to collapse in deep despair, grief, and paralysis. He loses his courage completely, throws down his weapons and refuses to go into battle. His eyes fills with tears; he calls out for help.

In response to Arjuna's desperate situation and cry for guidance, the Self reveals Itself in the form of his chariot driver, Krishna, who gradually shows himself to be Vishnu, Lord of the universe.12 Krishna begins to guide Arjuna, saying:

Whence this lifeless dejection, Arjuna, in this hour, the hour of trial? Strong men know not despair, Arjuna; this wins neither heaven nor earth. Fall not into degrading weakness, for this becomes not a man who is a man. Throw off this ignoble discouragement, and arise like a fire that burns all before it.13

As Arjuna's spiritual teacher, Krishna explains his infinite nature and encourages Arjuna to free himself from karma and the grip of the senses by surrendering to the deeper Self:

From the world of the senses, Arjuna, comes heat and comes cold, and pleasure and pain. They come and they go: they are transient. Arise above them, strong soul. The man whom these cannot move, whose soul is one, beyond pleasure and pain, is worthy of life in eternity.14

Leave all things behind, and come to me for thy salvation. I will make thee free from the bondage of sins. Fear no more.15

Instead of letting Arjuna sink down into his own defeat when he meets his life's biggest challenge, Krishna inspires him to rise up and meet it in a way that liberates him from this and all karmic situations. Krishna instructs Arjuna to solve the dilemma by letting karma go its natural course while simultaneously relating to it in a state of unshakable surrender to the fundamental energy of life. With this teaching, Arjuna attains an understanding that gives him the peace and strength to carry out his role in the battle in a liberated and open state, without attachment to the outcome. He gains an unlimited perspective, and an experience of unity and non-attachment.

The Bhagavad Gita illustrates both the importance of surrendering to the Self and the significance of the teacher's role in the liberation process. It also makes clear how a practitioner should relate to an authentic guide in order to get the greatest reward through the exchange. Further, the poem can inspire us toward an inner attitude and logic that will serve us well when we face our own difficult challenges and choices in the course of our lives. This attitude is nicely summarized in the preface to the poem:

We must and shall act, but we shall not bind ourselves to our actions through egoistical motives and thus act manipulating based on what is useful for ourselves. We shall let go of the fruit of our actions. The action itself shall be the goal. In that way, we free ourselves from the consequences.16

Balance

Are we doomed to remain mired in the biological imperatives we were born with, and the social patterns and psychic scars we have acquired? Are we destined to remain limited by our ego, to live in tension, to continue chasing after and clinging to what we think we need to be happy and fulfilled in this life? Or is it possible for us, like Arjuna, to liberate ourselves from the web of karma and enter a totally different dimension of life experience? These are the central questions that every spiritual tradition and religion always attempt to address and provide answers to, and which holy men and women from various traditions have managed to fulfill in practice.

We are all on the battlefield of our own lives every day. The situations and challenges we face are not necessarily as dramatic as those facing Arjuna in the Bhagavad Gita, but we must all continually make conscious choices in our lives, and it is easy to become overwhelmed and paralyzed by the tension and pressure we confront on a daily basis. The same solution that Krishna revealed to Arjuna can also be applied to our lives and circumstances.

For example, if we are in a love relationship that, for whatever reasons, has become dysfunctional, we may descend into a state of faint-heartedness at the thought of either having to leave the relationship or stay in it. In the first case, we bring our partner and ourselves a lot of pain by breaking up. In the other case, by remaining in an apparently hopeless situation, we continue to suffer. As the Bhagavad Gita makes clear, there is a third possibility: to rise above the faint-heartedness by opening to and surrendering into the Self within, thereby allowing a deeper inner balance to assert itself. In that more balanced state, not only does the right choice usually show itself clearly after some time, but we acquire the deeper inner strength necessary to carry out that choice, without undue anxiety about the consequences.

If we make conscious choices and take action in this way, without attachment to ego, the results tend to be much more beneficial for all involved than if ego clinging overwhelmed us and we acted in an agitated, desperate, and unbalanced state. There is far greater likelihood we could remain friends with the person we choose to leave, if we choose to break. If we choose to stay and work on the relationship, our chances of fully improving it are far greater if we make that decision in a non-attached state. It is the inner attitude and state we are in while making and executing the choice that is decisive.

This kind of decision-making can have a major influence at home in relation to a spouse, significant other, children, relatives, and friends, or in relation to our workplace or different social roles we are engaged in. In all situations that we encounter in these arenas, it is very easy to get stuck acting from chasing and clinging, from tension, patterns, projections, and illusions. We can avoid this through conscious inner work, by not reacting to what we think violates or insults us in some way. Instead, we simply take refuge in the deeper Self, so that our responses arise from inner balance, peace, strength, and compassion. Instead of pouring gasoline on the fire, we allow the Self to manage it. In that way, the possibility of engaging others with cooperation, meaningful and clear communication, intimacy, creativity, effectiveness, and growth becomes a genuine reality.

It is challenging to transcend the ego, to open to life without clinging to expectations, and to see things from the perspective of the Self. The web of karma is very difficult to become free of. Many people are very attached to the experiences they have had and the patterns and situations that have formed in them. Whether we feel that we are not good enough in relation to others or that we are better than everyone else, both of these extremes are ego and represent limiting inner attitudes. To have an open attitude is to let go of all extremes and simply be who we really are, centered in the Self, reposing in the inner posture called *maha mudra*. Maintaining this inner attitude does not require, deny or prevent feeling. On the contrary, many powerful feelings emerge when we are deeply connected to the Self. We are filled with the joy of life in all its manifestations, from pain and grief to love, gratitude, and compassion. We become much warmer and more fully human, less reactionary or cold.

When it comes to avoiding entanglement in the web of karma, it is our inner attitude and purpose behind what we think, say, and do that is most important. Even if we inadvertently act in a way that contributes to an unexpected, even very painful consequence, this will not further entangle us in karma so long as our action arises from an inner posture and purpose of genuine compassion for others and surrender to the Self.

The inner attitude required for liberation demands an unconditional love of life as a whole, to its fundamental energy. Toward the end of his life Rudi was asked about the difference between consciousness and ego. In his reply, he described two distinctly different ways to live:

To do things in tune with the basic consciousness is love; to do things with an ego focus is a kind of rape. Ego takes the credit for things that happen and beats its chest with pride. When we are immersed in consciousness, we know that everything that happens has deeper causes than ego, and we stand in humble gratitude to God.17

In Tune with the Self

What Rudi describes in the quote above can be called the logic of the Self. As we make contact with the fundamental energy, its voice compels us to live our life not from the logic of materialism and temporary concerns but from the logic of openness, humility, gratitude, and compassion. This logic can never be discovered by struggling with questions arising from ego but is discovered only by learning to let go of all ego concerns. The logic of the Self transforms fear, doubt, and insecurity into courage and creativity; pain and anger become unlimited well-being. When we allow the logic of the Self to begin to inform our life, we discover that all the changes, challenges, and difficulties we go through are opportunities to discover more about our deepest potential for liberation.

Maintaining this highest perspective means focusing on the spiritual and eternal rather than on the temporary needs and rewards of the ego. The highest perspective has its own built-in rewards, far surpassing anything that the logic of the ego can bring about. In letting go of our lower self, we learn to immerse ourselves in the core of everything that has form. We learn to recognize and experience everything as energy and flow, which allows us to relate to the world from the widest possible perspective and deepest reality. We learn to relate to everyone and everything from a state of liberated wisdom, meaning we move through every situation in our life in a state of true recognition and compassion at all levels, from the most concrete and physical to the most subtle and non-material. The purpose of all our actions is then simply to serve, wherever and however we can, and do our part in contributing to inner growth and liberation. Universal power is set in motion and becomes available for this when we live according to the logic of the Self.

Other Traditions

The logic of the Self is clearly emphasized in many other traditions, though that specific term may not be used to describe it. Taoism, classic Hinduism, Sufism, and Christianity all express the importance of following such logic. The Taoist master Lao-tzu, for instance, has put it like this:

A wise man does not hoard. The more he uses in the service of others, the more he has for himself. The more he gives to his fellow human beings, the more he has for himself.18

Lao-tzu says here that by giving away everything, you lose nothing. Mysteriously, you get back more than you give.

India's well-known spiritual leader Mahatma Gandhi exemplified, by the way he lived his life, a deep commitment to living according to the logic of the Self, emphasizing surrender and service. During many instances of nonviolent protest and fasting, often with his life on the line, he demonstrated his willingness to give everything, even his own life, for what he perceived as the highest truth. His purpose was to consciously offer himself while at the same time not harming others. On the subject of serving others, he said this:

Service can have no meaning unless one takes pleasure in it. When it is done for show or for fear of public opinion, it stunts the man and crushes his spirit. Service which is rendered without joy helps neither the servant nor the served.19

The Persian Sufi poet and spiritual teacher Jelaluddin Rumi is revered for having lived his life according to the logic of the Self. He wrote many beautiful poems about this experience, such as this one, which clearly and elegantly summarizes the importance of surrendering to unconditional love in order to live a spiritual life:

Love is reckless, not reason.

Reason seeks profit.

Love comes on strong, consuming herself, unabashed.

Yet in the midst of suffering

Love proceeds like a millstone,

hard surfaced and straight-forward.

Having died to self-interest,

she risks everything and asks for nothing.

Love gambles away every gift God bestows.

Without cause God gave us being;

without cause give it back again.

Gambling yourself away is beyond any religion.

Religion seeks grace and favor,

But those who gamble these away are God's favorites,

For they neither put God to the test nor knock at the

door of gain and loss.[20]

Christianity, too, invokes the logic of the Self as a central theme. To turn the other cheek, for instance, is to demonstrate that external events have no bearing on our inner state. It represents the sacrifice of the ego in order to achieve spiritual liberation. The single most important symbol in Christianity of the logic of the Self and its inherent reward is, of course, the crucifixion and resurrection of Jesus Christ. To understand the story of Jesus's death on the cross is to see it not as punishment but as a conscious process of spiritual liberation attained through self-sacrifice. Whether or not the story of his life and death is literally true or not seems less important than its fundamental message: that it is possible to liberate oneself and experience spiritual rebirth through deep surrender to a deeper reality than the ego. The most important and powerful aspect of the story of Christ is that it can inspire us to make that same logic a living reality in our own lives, here and now.

To live a life of selfless service based on the logic of the Self is much easier said than done. It runs counter to the values of popular culture, common sense, and the intuition that springs out of biological imperatives. It is like swimming against the stream and the spirit of the times. In the process, we might lose friends and acquaintances, but we will also attract new people and situations in our life from the deeper inner state we are in. If we dare to surrender and offer our lower self without reservation, we discover that this action leads to deep inner peace, energy, and well-being. It liberates us. It contributes to increasing immersion in the fundamental consciousness, where we gain access to profound inner strength, joy, and freedom.

8

CULTIVATION

What lies at the core of our being—our individual soul—can be seen as an inner seed of liberation. The seed within the core of a human being represents an individuated frequency of the Self, the infinite Soul. Like all seeds in nature, if cultivated properly, it contains the potential to grow and unfold into something ripe and nourishing. Within a human being, this seed can develop into a spiritual being with the capacity to provide inner nourishment and inspiration to others. Based on its frequency and inherent natural characteristics, in combination with the care and nourishment it receives, the seed grows into an authentic spiritual being, unique in form and expression, yet one with the Self.

A shell covers our inner seed, just like any seed in nature. The shell covering an individual soul is made up of traces and scars from the past, including past lives. This shell is the veiling force, in the form of the ego, with its illusions, tensions, blocks, and limiting patterns. It is the web of karma that we are caught in, preventing the fundamental energy from arising and unfolding within our awareness. It prevents our inner system from functioning to its full potential.

In order to break through this shell, the inherent power of the universal soul needs to be awakened within us. For that to happen, being connected with a teacher is very helpful. It also requires that we sit down daily to give attention to our inner mechanism. This is analogous to watering our inner seed and making sure it gets enough light.

A common experience among people who develop some inner growth is that they become increasingly saturated with the qualities arising through consistent practice and contact with the Self: centeredness, concentration, joy, clarity, openness, grounding, inner strength, balance, well-being, creativity, and compassion. One of our greatest challenges as practitioners is to not become complacent related to ego at any point in the growth process. Instead of becoming satisfied or clinging to any attainments we may have achieved, it is far better to continually surrender those into a higher state of consciousness, all the while maintaining intensity of focus on the wish for continued inner growth. Only by working in this way is it possible to become the best human being that we can be in this life. Inner growth is a lifelong process.

Growing Pains

It is often painful when the shell surrounding the soul breaks or dissolves. Periods of boundary dissolution, transformation, and increased energy flow are not often comfortable or peaceful experiences. Pain and discomfort are natural and necessary aspects of inner development, as in all growth in nature. One way to understand this dimension of pain and discomfort is to view it simply as the friction between our universal and individual aspects, as the two engage each other and gradually become unified. For example, a person may, due to upbringing emphasizing the need to always be safe and not exposed to danger, have a deep resistance to and fear of entering a state without boundaries. This individual tendency will create a sense of friction between the state that the person is used to and the boundless state that opens up in a conscious effort to merge with the Self.

Growth is experienced as painful because of inherent resistance to change. This resistance is evident not only in relation to spiritual growth but any growth that may occur as a result of natural challenges, such as the breakup of a close relationship, the death of a friend or relative, or other strong life situations. When we lose someone we deeply love, it can lead to either becoming stuck in resistance and undigested pain or to a significant increase in energy and a broadening of perspective. The latter happens by consciously letting go and gradually digesting the pain. If we do not respond consciously to the challenges in life, we inevitably experience the effects of that avoidance in the form of numbness, depression, anger, and other forms of tension. We also see the effects of such lack of digestion reflected in the people around us.

Even without an inner practice, some people somehow manage to absorb the pain of a challenging situation and grow through it, becoming bigger, stronger, more passionate and open, with an expanded repertoire of feelings, as well as greater freedom of thought and action. Others do not manage to let go and become more closed, knotted up, and limited. This inner state is often reflected in people's facial expressions and posture, in the way they stand, walk, sit, breathe, and talk. They appear weighed down by life. Their faces tend to look pinched and frozen, as if their hearts were incapable of opening to life. They may take on a slightly bent-over posture, with the shoulders pulled in tight, as if to protect the heart. Their breathing is often more irregular and shallower than normal, and their voices weak and unclear. It is difficult to observe oneself or a fellow human being in such a sad condition. Fortunately, it is never too late to begin a practice and a process that improve this state.

Cultivating our inner life doesn't mean that we no longer experience the pain of being human. Rather, it means that we develop the capacity to relax deeply in order to let the pain dissolve enough that we can digest and draw nourishment from it. The key is to stop struggling against the pain and to consciously relate to it as a natural and digestible aspect of life, as the tough love of the Self. We then find that the energy of the pain is transformed into deeper gratitude and expanded understanding, wisdom, and compassion. Tension, on the other hand, represents frozen pain; there is no flow. Tension increases suffering by crystallizing into solid blocks within us, creating big inner and outer difficulties. If we continuously push it under the carpet it starts to rot, creating more pain and suffering.

Deep Roots

When the shell of a seed that has been planted breaks and begins to grow, it first sends out roots through which it takes in nourishment from the soil.

Eventually, a stem emerges and stretches upward to break through the surface toward the light, toward the more subtle and powerful nourishment of direct exposure to the sun. This also happens to us as human beings when we practice and become more conscious of the energy flow at the core of our existence. The fundamental energy breaks through the shell and establishes deep roots connected with the core of our being, the earth, and everything we come from, and then stretches toward the light above.

That does not mean that we break with our familial and social roots but that we transform them into inner roots through conscious practice. We use these roots to draw nourishment from the very tensions and patterns inherent in family and social dynamics, and from the life we have, here and now. This is primarily done by maintaining an open, centered, and surrendered inner attitude, dissolving and releasing the energy that lies crystallized in the chakra system as tensions, blocks, and patterns. The energy is then circulated within, down the front and up the back.

Working in this way, we find that we can use all situations—both those that formed us in the past and those we are dealing with in the present—as fuel for growth. In a sense, we are lifted up into the light, to the universal dimension of the deeper Self, by this fuel that becomes increased flow. In the process, we sacrifice our tensions and patterns. In opening to the universal dimension within everything present in our life, an uplifting and liberating energy begins to unfold. This energy has its own inherent intelligence, its own way of developing, and the particular fruits that appear in us over time are natural expressions of our deepest potential and the work we do. As we deepen our practice, we become increasingly marked by this energy, and by the simple awareness of powerfully expanded presence and potential. We become more joyful, more fulfilled human beings. We gain a greater capacity to feel and give of ourselves. Gradually, we fully recognize that the light above and all around us is the same as the light that is within us.

We cannot hide behind the shell that covers our soul and expect to grow inside. Remaining trapped in self-pity by thinking and reinforcing such thoughts as, "Poor me, my life is so much worse than everyone else's; I'm so special in my suffering," is an all-too-common way to hide behind the shell. Likewise, hiding behind either self-rejection or arrogance, expressed in thoughts like, *"I'm not pretty enough, smart enough, rich enough, etc.,"* or *"I'm so much better than everyone else that I don't have to work inside,"* guarantees against inner growth. So does looking to the outside for something or someone to blame every time something we do not like happens. If we do that, the soul is never revealed to us and we forfeit the possibility of experiencing glimpses of and union with the Self. On the contrary, going deeply within and letting go of all such thinking while opening fully to the potential that lies buried behind the shell, within the core of the seed, allows the seed to open and grow.

Ripening

As our inner shell begins to crack or dissolve and the energy unfolds, life around us also begins to change. Situations, people, and things may fall away from us as a natural part of the growth process, and new people and situations appear. Even though it may be very difficult to let go of what we are accustomed to, consciously allowing this to happen, especially when everything is trying to tell us that a situation or person is ready to fall away from us, is necessary.

Everyone has a tendency to hang on to what they already have in life, even though some of what they hold on to may be as lifeless as dead branches on a tree. This clinging occurs not only in inner practice but also in everyday life. One example is the case of a woman hanging on to a violent husband or boyfriend who abuses her in many ways. Often, women choose to stay in such a relationship because it is easier to remain in a familiar situation than to move into the unknown, even when the known situation is very harmful and not at all nourishing. Another example may be clinging to a job that creates so much inner stress that it results in serious sickness. Listening with the heart to what is really happening and the action that it calls for is important in such cases.

Practitioners who manage to surrender, let go, and digest their pain generally experience a rebirth afterward in which new life opportunities emerge. Parts of them fall away, and new shoots that can bear fruit begin to appear. At this stage, many people begin to be fascinated by the person they start becoming through inner work and growth.

As we develop greater inner strength, capacity, energy, and self-confidence, it is easy to get confused about how to use these newly acquired attractive qualities. Ego can take over at any moment, leading us to prematurely pick, eat, and offer the small green fruits that appear before they have a chance to fully ripen. They may taste a little sour even to us, but we are so impressed by the fact that they are *our* fruits, *our* qualities, that we feel compelled to offer them as if they were sweet and ripe. This is a kind of spiritual arrogance that needs to be surrendered. People actually get sick to their stomach from eating unripe fruit; the same is true of human qualities that are stuck in ego.

It is much better to give the ripening process the time it needs in order to complete itself rather than willfully charging ahead with the illusion of ripeness. This demands a lot of patient inner work and non-attachment. If we succeed in maintaining our focus on the wish to grow and surrender over a long enough time, then our state of being gradually becomes increasingly powerful yet humble and sweet, despite the pain and challenges that are an integral part of the growth process. In the early stages of our development, it is best to give of ourselves in the simplest, most practical ways to the people and situations in our immediate environment and to be patient and realistic when it comes to grander, more challenging forms of service. These things come in due time, as we ripen enough to handle them appropriately. It is the fully ripened sweetness—and the energy, wisdom, and compassion that come with it—that is of real value and can nourish and inspire others.

Growth Spurts

If a plant does not receive water it dies, regardless of how large it has become. Maintaining focus on inner practice even when there does not seem to be much happening as a result is essential. Often, when it seems most difficult to sit down and practice, that is precisely when we are on the brink of a breakthrough. Spiritual growth, like physical growth, usually happens in bursts or spurts. There can be long periods without noticeable growth or change, then suddenly a breakthrough happens, and a deeper experience of tension release and an expanded realization and range of possibilities occur.

This natural phenomenon of growth spurts has also been observed through scientific research into the physical growth process of infants. In a study by Michelle Lampl at the University of Pennsylvania some years ago, it was found that infants between three and fifteen months old grew an average of half an inch in twenty-four hours, and then did not grow at all in a period from two to twenty-eight days.21 Lampl also noticed that a few days prior to a growth spurt, the infant became very hungry, irritable, and agitated.

This growth process parallels the process of inner growth in us. Day after day, for weeks or months, we can sit and work inside without experiencing anything significant. We then have a tendency to become impatient, agitated, and irritable, and we may hear an inner voice say, *"Why am I doing this? I'm not really getting anywhere."* In order to get beyond this mental obstruction, we need to discern this as the voice of the ego and consciously work past its invitation to give up. Then, when we least expects it, a growth spurt occurs: a block of tensions melts, we gain a deeper realization, with the gratitude, joy, and expansion that accompany it.

Pruning and Support

As described earlier, feedback, guidance, and support from a capable teacher can help at critical points in the ripening process. The teacher provides these simply through his or her presence, as well as through words and other means. At times, there is a need for a kind of pruning that can contribute to a growth spurt. The ego is blind to anything but itself when it dominates our awareness. It is totally captured by its experience of itself and its concerns. It is, therefore, difficult to know and admit to ourselves when we are locked in ego, particularly when we are in the middle of an emotional or situational storm.

In order for feedback and pruning to be effective and beneficial, it is important that the practitioner consciously opens to receive it, regardless of how deeply it goes against the grain of what he or she believes about him- or herself. It means that the practitioner needs to be on guard in relation to the defensive or attacking voice of the ego, and let go of it as quickly and deeply as possible as it occurs. If we do the inner work to stay open and let go, it is usually enough to just be in inner contact with the teacher. Through that contact we usually discover our own ego tendencies and patterns. If we listen deeply enough, we can hear the voice of the Self: *"Here your ego is in control and reacting,"* it might say. *"Why do you think like that? Why do you react that way? Why do you do this? That doesn't contribute to your growth."* Even if we do not hear such a voice, we may consciously remember the words of a teacher, who may have said similar things, or who we know would probably ask similar challenging questions about our ego focus. In response to these challenges, we simply follow guidance from the deeper reality by letting go and by changing our attitude and behavior. In this way, we align ourselves with the Self and allow *it* to be in control.

There are, of course, times when the teacher clearly sees the necessity for a stronger medicine in the form of powerful, clear feedback, as Krishna gave to Arjuna on the battlefield. Such feedback is given to help us deepen our inner work. It is necessary pruning. The teacher sees the possibility for a growth spurt in the practitioner through a particular situation or exchange, and does what he or she can to contribute to that growth and ripening. If the practitioner does not open to the teacher's feedback as such, but instead reacts from ego, then the shell around his or her soul hardens even more, creating a thicker wall rather than increased flow between practitioner and teacher, and between the practitioner and his or her own experience of a deeper inner reality.

In addition to giving challenging feedback at times, a teacher also provides support where and when it is necessary and possible. As a spiritual gardener, the teacher metaphorically places supportive stakes in the ground under heavy branches in order for the trees, bushes, and plants in the garden to grow correctly and for flowers to blossom and berries and fruits to ripen. A teacher's extra support may come in many forms, from simply giving a practitioner more attention, pointing out opportunities, offering suggestions for the best use of the person's resources and abilities, or giving guidance concerning specific life situations. The teacher does not tell practitioners what to do but gives guidance designed to open them to new possibilities and to help them be aware of the consequences of various directions and decisions. Such support, like pruning, helps us grow and ripen as human and spiritual beings.

9

UNCONDITIONAL LOVE

The more I do the Rising Energy Practice, the clearer it becomes that unconditional love is the main point of it all. It is not *falling in love*, but loving life itself with all its expressions, in an open state of non-attachment. Surrender is the key factor in reaching a state where this unconditional love can exist. We let go of all the noise and distraction in our life and see through it to its core. If we are stuck in ego there really cannot be unconditional love. There can only be a kind of business. I give you this and you give me that. There is some subtle or not so subtle agreement that I pay you and you give me something agreed upon in return for it.

Ego attachment has no place in the process of going into a state where love springs forth as a natural expression. By letting go of all agendas we can be in that deeper state while being engaged with family, relationships, work in the world, and with friends. We can have that sense of love everywhere, but it takes conscious inner work and a looking through the ego and identity aspects into the Self so that we can relate from its inherent qualities. No matter what obstacles to love show up in us in the context of any relationship, in any situation, we can always go to that natural state in us where love lives and we can always invite others to share in that. We don't always get the response we would like, we do not always get back the love that we feel and invite others to share in, but whenever we do not, we have to let go of that.

The world is what it is. People are caught to various degrees in their identity issues. It is natural for these issues to come up. When they come up they can be related to as opportunities to let go. We can say *"what can I do in this situation"*, rather than saying to ourselves: *"This man is crazy, or this woman is not nice to me. What's wrong with these people?"* All of a sudden we are totally involved in judging. If we instead turn our attention inward and say: *"What about me? Why am I reacting the way I do to this?"* Maybe if we really let go, something in us could spontaneously rise up that would allow us to communicate in such a way that the other person would open to us. Even if the person still does not open up, at least we know that we have done our best.

*

A natural and complete transformation of awareness happens as a result of deep, regular Rising Energy Practice over time. I have experienced that over many years and through many phases of life, and I have seen it in many practitioners. In this practice we are not just trying to live with less stress. We are digging deeply within ourselves for extraordinary life experience, marked by immersion in deeper awareness. This is the greatest challenge we can take on, but it is also the most rewarding.

When we open to a deeper state, compassion for ourselves and others naturally arises. The more we can open to face our own peculiarities and those of others without judging, the more we will be able to share in a real experience of love. The exchange we have with others will then be marked by a sense of energy flow and underlying Oneness, and by wisdom and compassion. There isn't anything more precious in this life than that. Family is great, relationships are great, and money is great; fame is great and career is great, but all these things are relatively small compared to the experience of being in touch with the deeper energy and potential for unconditional love at the core of us and everyone. Being in touch with that deeper energy and potential makes all aspects of life much more fulfilling because it brings unconditional love into it.

All people have tensions and obstacles in life, functioning like clouds covering the light of awareness at the core of being. Everyone has a family history, challenges in relation to work, and patterns of thinking and reacting. The tension and obstacles in us related to all these areas of life, which are all aspects of the veiling effect, become more visible than ever in the process of our inner work, simply because they get energized with our attention. This intensification is necessary in order for us to know exactly what to let go of. If we can learn to use these tensions and obstacles to work more deeply inside, then we may discover that all of it, even the most challenging experience, is essentially infinite potential, unconditional love and creative energy at the core.

Emotion as Springboard

If we get tense about something and feel a strong emotion of anger or disappointment toward ourselves or another person, that emotion can be used as a springboard to a deeper awareness. If we do our practice in response to this strong emotion, going into our breath and chakras, allowing ourselves to experience our emotion fully while at the same time relaxing and opening deeply, we find that a fine energy experience of release and gratitude emerges at the core of the emotion. We feel our anger and tightness, but at the same time we work to feel into the core of it where the energy flow can be released. We feel our heart and chakra system open and allow the anger and tension to melt in that opening. It may not happen on the first breath, but it will gradually occur if we stay with it long enough. Doing this inner work builds inner psychic muscles. It builds a mechanism that can dissolve our tensions and obstacles.

Any strong emotion can be used as the springboard to a deeper energy flow and awareness. If we move our attention from being stuck in thoughts about the emotion and instead feel into our heart and the chakras below, a different experience emerges. We circulate our attention with our breath inside, down the front and up the back. We allow the still-points between the breaths to open up and become doorways into a wide open space vibrating with unlimited potential. We sit, observe and let go. What emerges in us as a result of this inner process is a deep sense of release.

We allow ourselves to feel a transformation from being stuck in thoughts and emotions to simply feeling the flow of energy which thoughts and emotions are rooted in and made of. Emotions are just energy under pressure, and so is any kind of doubt, resistance or confusion. We can bring our attention into our psychic system and just ask, open and let go instead

106

of being stuck in our mind, going through things again and again, analyzing and judging,

When tension and resistance are released tears might start flowing and we may feel some spontaneous tension release movement (kriyas). We will definitely feel something shifting inside. In the end we will very likely feel lighter and relieved, like a burden has fallen from our shoulders. This is very gratifying and uplifting.

When we commit to go more deeply into ourselves, the universe usually presents some ways to test us in the process of moving in that direction. For example, we may find ourselves in a very challenging situation that requires a lot of our attention, and we may at the same time be at a stage of a growth cycle where we feel that we are not making any progress and that the obstacles facing us are overwhelming. This may cause us to be discouraged from going on with the inner work. We may feel like we are in the middle of a tunnel without an end in sight, and we may lose our motivation to move on through whatever is facing us to its conclusion. We may fail to rise up and deal effectively with what is testing us. An inner voice of might arise inside: *"Are you still going to stay open and flowing and continue to move forward, even with these difficult challenges, or are you going to get stuck here?"* It is necessary to allow ourselves to feel the tension, imbalance, resistance and strong emotional reaction to such tests, but not to get stuck in any of it. Instead, we let go inside as deeply as possible and continue to move forward in the practice, step by step, so that what needs to die can do so and so that new life can manifest. We develop stronger psychic muscles inside in the process, and we increase our capacity to hold awareness of a wide open inner space that can transform and dissolve tension and obstacles. By doing so, new things open within and around us.

Extraordinary Life

What we do in the Rising Energy Practice or in any serious deep practice that is done regularly over enough time, is allowing ourselves to be transformed from having what may be called an ordinary life experience to having an extraordinary one. The Taoist tradition talks of "drowning in the dust of everyday experience." All the different phases of life have their difficulties and challenges that it is easy to drown in. Particularly as adults, people often tend to just go through life on automatic pilot. They often do what everyone else around them is doing and what their parents and surroundings have been teaching them about how to live. This is the least challenging but also the least satisfying way to respond to life as an adult.

By learning to be immersed in a deeper state of being while going through the different phases of life, particularly as an adult, the phases all become freer and more satisfying, both for us and for people around us. We start to have a more extraordinary life experience that can be shared with others. We become better students, workers, managers, husbands, mothers, fathers, etc. because we get a deeper sense of joy, energy and purpose through our inner growth. We can go through these stages with some contact with and understanding of the power of inner work and of letting go into unconditional love.

Whatever the particular of our life, we can get better at living it with joy, energy and compassion. We can learn to live with less fear of change and death because we taste the infinity which is beyond life and death. When we taste that infinity, we know with our whole being that there is something beyond the problems associated with our physical, mental and emotional life. We know that unconditional love is real. Life and death then are not as frightening as before. We know that we are something deeper than all the superficial aspects of our identity, that we are something deeper and more essential than the limitations of our physical, mental and emotional existence. We know it in our deepest awareness and recognition, not only with our rational mind.

What can be realized in the middle of any so called ordinary life sequence is that something more is available if we just reach for it and open to it. This requires, as a starting point, feeling a sense of deep dissatisfaction with the limitations of an ordinary life filled with repetition of old patterns of thinking, feeling and reacting. From that dissatisfaction, we can reach into a practice that suits us. Through it, we can gradually free ourselves from the limitations of the ordinary and rise into a life of extraordinary joy, energy and freedom.

As we work at it long enough, putting our sincere attention and effort into it, while letting go of whatever appears as obstacles to our quest, we gradually become what we are reaching for. We become the Oneness that we wished for as a seeker; we become that unconditional love, that experience of joy, energy and compassion that we have had glimpses of as an initiate and practitioner. We realize that infinite potential filled with creative energy and unconditional love is all we are. There is nothing we need to chase after, and there is nothing to cling to. We already have it all and it cannot leave us unless we turn our attention away from it.

10

FREEDOM

In connection with spiritual practices, the word "freedom" refers to an uplifted, wide-open state of being. It means living immersed in the Self, continuously rising above ego attachment. In Western culture, however, "freedom" usually implies something quite different. While it can easily have different meanings in different contexts, there has been a growing tendency, ever since the hippie movement of the late 1960s and early 1970s, to use the word "freedom" to describe a kind of nihilism or selfishness, what Henrik Ibsen in his famous play Peer Gynt called being *"enough unto myself."*22 This is not the freedom that is the goal and result of inner practice.

While the hippie movement had many positive aspects, especially its idealism, openness, and resistance to using war as a way to exert power and solve conflicts, the freedom it proclaimed was, at best, very limited, and therefore not freedom at all. Focused primarily on illusions, the freedom it proclaimed was a mentality that excluded most perspectives other than that of ego satisfaction. This mentality lives on today even in alternative circles, where a common notion is that a person can free themselves from the web of karma by being his or her own inner teacher. The belief that "I am enough unto myself" is very limiting. Those who claim not to need anyone else's support and guidance often insist on diagnosing their own inner state and creating their own treatment program. For this reason, people who are taken with this mentality often avoid any challenges to their ego, or they invest a lot of time and energy constructing arguments about why they are right and others are wrong. It is very difficult, if not impossible, to become immersed in the Self through this approach, which ultimately leads to anxiety, paranoia, separateness, and conflicts. In short: it leads to continued and increasing entanglement in the web of karma.

True freedom means liberation from the constraints of the ego and the web of karma, and it includes a willingness and capacity to let go of ego boundaries. Such freedom is called *moksha* in Sanskrit. Real freedom includes a willingness to be wrong, to not know, to be open to different perspectives, to be responsible and disciplined, to learn new things, and to surrender to the deeper reality of the Self. The intense yearning for this type of freedom opens the way for total immersion in the deeper Self. It dissolves questions and conflicts surrounding *my thing* and *your thing*. It emphasizes *our thing* in the broadest, most universal sense. This life is *our thing*. The love that we experience together is *our thing*. The Self is *our thing*. This fundamental reality of stillness and creative energy, and not the superficial differences between us, is the most meaningful. We have been given the free will to choose to focus on and to fully give ourselves to this reality.

Guided by the Self

If we want liberation from the constraints of the ego, a much broader perspective than that which is tied to our biological imperatives and our personal and social patterns is called for. In order to experience the qualities inherent in contact with the Self, our ego attachments need to dissolve. This is not to be understood as a repression or denial of our biology, individuality, or connection with social patterns but simply as freedom from those factors in the sense that they no longer hinder us from discovering a deeper level of experience. In this way, the possibility of total freedom opens up.

When we get caught in situations and relationships, it is necessary to let go of our personal agendas. The only means to free ourselves from the complex network of desires we carry within us is to surrender. To consciously let go of our own agenda is to give in to the reality of the Self. This is not the same as resignation or giving in to someone else's agenda. Surrender is a conscious, self-healing act requiring that we simply rise, again and again, above the constraints of our own desires. We let go into the deeper Self, wherein all possibilities reside. Then, a totally different feeling, atmosphere, and flow emerge from within to extend out toward others and into all the external dynamics of our life. This means allowing the universal energy, and not the ego, to guide our movements and interactions. Far more creative and compassionate acts and initiatives naturally arise in this liberated atmosphere, and more unifying solutions and directions assert themselves.

If others are not inspired or able to cooperate in this open and positive environment, then at least we know that we have done our best, and have not caused more entanglement in karma for ourselves and others. Like Arjuna on the battlefield, we have done what we can and ought to do. We have acted to the best of our ability, in tune with the will of our deeper inner being.

As we become immersed in the Self, we attract to ourselves whatever is needed to dissolve the deeper karmic traces, scars, and knots buried within us, including those from past lives. We actually attract certain people, relationships, and situations to ourselves precisely to create the opportunities to dissolve the karmic knots and traces of the past that are represented and made visible by them. Such relationships and situations provide the very possibility of allowing the patterns buried within them to dissolve through deepening practice, surrender, and selfless service.

It is necessary to take responsibility for and give nourishment to every situation we attract by being willing to fulfill whatever the situation demands of us, in a state of openness and surrender. To serve these situations requires that we serve and give of ourselves to them. We do what we can to serve these situations without clinging to the outcome. To the degree that we manage this, the karma within such situations dissolves, becoming liberated energy that we can use to accelerate our spiritual growth. In this way, some relationships and situations become so profoundly transformed that they contribute to our further inner ripening and freedom. Other relationships and situations fall away because we have given all we can to them, and they have given all they can in return. We are finished with them. It usually requires many years of hard work to transcend the inner and outer obstacles in our life and to build an inner mechanism strong enough to maintain regular immersion in the deepest state of consciousness. When we are sincerely focused and anchored in this state, we can receive ongoing nourishment from it, regardless of whatever else is going on in our lives. We are simply aware that we *are* the consciousness in which everything unfolds. This is a magnificent and boundless state of inner well-being that is something to be very grateful for.

Vibrating As the Self

One of the most amazing results of inner work is that over time, as we regularly open our heart and circulate energy in the chakra system, the subtle presence and fine vibration frequency of the Self builds within us. It ripens within over time as a result of doing the practice with depth and devotion. To the extent that we have given of ourselves to the process of becoming immersed in this fine vibration while living in the physical body, the vibration continues even after the dissolution of the physical body. This is the opposite of becoming a hungry ghost after death, clinging to the earthly plane on which we no longer belong. Just as a hungry ghost can somehow live on as an unfulfilled and disturbed vibration, an uplifting and nourishing vibration can live on after the physical body has dissolved, as a service to all those who come after. This is why many people find it uplifting and inspiring to visit sites where great inner beings have lived and passed on, even though the visitors never knew or had contact with these people when they were in their physical bodies.

The being we become by investing our life force in inner growth has the capacity to function by itself, as a direct emanation of the fundamental energy. No longer ruled by attractions, prejudices, or repulsions, the state of being attained through deep inner work over time is a state without boundaries, wide open and aware. Immersed in that state, we have the capacity to offer a boundless presence and vibration to others. This is accomplished not by retreating from the world but by embracing all of life in a state of non-attachment. By maintaining contact with this state, we have much more to give to the situations we meet in life, and to the inscrutable mystery that meets us after death.

All human beings have the right to live and die in that state. Nourishment received from contact with teachers, and the work we do in connection with them, completes the inner growth process, making complete liberation in this lifetime a genuine possibility. After death, a person liberated in life remains as a tangible vibration that can nourish others.

To achieve a liberated inner state, whatever vibratory tone and strength it assumes, is the best thing we can do for our descendants, who are not only our biological children or direct family. All who remain here after we leave the physical body are our descendants, especially those we have a deep inner bond with in this life. In actuality, neither our biological children nor people who practice meditation with us are *our* children. They are children of the Self, given to us by Consciousness to care for while they have a need for nourishment and support. We do not own them; they are temporary gifts, on loan from the Self and endowed with their own life force. Our role as guides to inner transformation or as physical parents is to give of our inner Self and allow those we guide to develop according to what is natural for them, without clinging to any particular outer form we might prefer.

The physical body is also a gift on loan from the Self, and our individuated inner growth is the best way to serve this deepest reality. To the extent that we achieve a spiritual presence, we can serve not just ourselves but everyone. In the texts of Kashmir Shaivism, it says that in liberating ourselves, we automatically contribute to the liberation of our closest family members in the generations that precede and follow us. I experienced this in relation to my mother while she lived. I hope it will be the case for those closest to me when I pass on, and for anyone who wants to use a connection with me for support.

If we are able to radiate a fine, uplifting, and liberating vibration while we live, and if we manage to maintain surrender to that vibration even as our physical body dissolves, then we are serving ourselves and others in the best way possible. We are anchored in a liberated state both in life and in death, which are but two sides of the same indivisible reality.

Daily Life

After a long period of growth, we begin to experience the influence of the growing inner being we are becoming on the different arenas we function in. By maintaining our focus and energy within, rather than externalizing it by leaking or projecting it outward, a different experience of life and the world around us becomes possible. We understand and relate to all tension, patterns, and blocks as crystallized energy. If we can be present to what is unfolding in the here and now, while at the same time maintaining awareness of the Self as the cause of it all, we have the ability to serve any situation in a much better and more compassionate way than if we were dominated by ego, reactionary patterns, and inner demons.

When we are centered and still in a simple, open inner state, a certain vibration extends itself to others that can uplift, inspire, and nourish them. To the extent that others are open to it by overcoming whatever resistance might arise in them, we become a conduit for the fundamental energy. Resistance is a natural response to the invitation to completely give in to the boundless nature of the Self. When the resistance is overcome, we find ourselves in the embrace of the fundamental energy.

As we grow, we begin to see many examples of the influence of our deeper state in our daily life. I noticed, for instance, some years ago when I held training sessions for industrial employees, that something more than what I brought in the form of concepts, information, and methods got exchanged and absorbed. While it was always important that course materials were of high quality, something deeper happened in the energy exchange, or flow, between the course participants and me. Most of the course participants reported feeling inspired and uplifted both during and after the course, in a way that would not have been possible solely through receiving factual information.

What happens in such interactions is that the energy field of the Self becomes part of the interactions and influences the atmosphere. When we surrender to it, the energy comes into our voice, facial expressions, and movements. This energy, which is unconditional love and respect, is present. It moves and creates a spark wherever there is an opening to receive it. People may not know exactly why they are positively affected, but it happens anyway.

Amazing Possibilities

The unfolding that occurs through inner practice and liberation is difficult, if not impossible, to foresee when we first begin, when we are still locked in our everyday limited awareness. As our practice matures and we have more contact with the core energy, the most surprising, intelligent and life-affirming events, amazing circumstances, and relationships begin to unfold. Things that were previously unimaginable begin to happen inside and around us.

While it is wonderful to experience the many newfound possibilities that open up both inside and around us as a result of practice, it is important to understand and remember that any attainments we achieve are temporary effects, signs of the creative power of the Self, gifts from that Self. These may be enjoyed and appreciated, but no such gifts are worthy of hanging on to as if they were the giver behind them. Only the fundamental source of the gifts, the dynamic potential and its energy, are eternal, and therefore must always remain the primary focus throughout life. The most amazing gift we receive in this life is the possibility of liberation from the self with a small 's' in order to become immersed in the Self with a capital 'S'. This gift brings with it amazing inner strength, well-being, freedom, and bliss.

Total Well-Being

As described earlier, the inner transformation required for liberation can be but may not be a peaceful process We may experience glimpses of immersion in the Self that are marked by simple presence and profound stillness, or we may experience strong energy movements as our inner system changes. As the dissolution process unfolds, the untying of all the karmic knots in our psychic system requires us to relive, on an energetic level, the experiences that led to the formation of the knots. This can be very disturbing and challenging at times. However, to the extent that we work correctly, the result is nothing short of liberating.

As the knots are loosened and untied, it becomes easier to breathe and experience the flow of energy within and between the chakras, as it moves down the front and up the back to the top of the head. The flow and spatial awareness in the entire psychic system deepens, and as this occurs, we gain the ability to discern between what contributes to our growth and what does not. We develop deeper compassion for and understanding of others. At last, we experience Oneness as the only continuous and ever-present reality, not just as a theory, wish, or glimpse, but as a total recognition. This whole process is analogous to peeling and eating a big onion. Focus, regular work, and some tears are necessary before we come to the sweet core. Patience, courage, and perseverance are essential. It is best to eat slowly and give ourselves plenty of time to digest.

In letting go of our prejudices, pre-set ideas, anxieties, and illusions, we allow what is natural, attuned to the Self, to awaken in and vibrate outward from us. This process brings about what is called *tapasya*, an inner burning of illusions and attachment to superficial, temporary things. This burning liberates us from our *samskaras*, our psychic scars and traces. Gradually, we rise above ego clinging and limitations. For most people who set out on this journey, it is a long and often painful process. To achieve the depth, power, and bliss of the Self requires letting go of surface entanglements, and a continuous striving for and surrender into a transcendent state.

Spiritual liberation means that we, through practice and revelation, come to recognize our true nature as pure Consciousness, as the Self. Continuous immersion in this recognition frees us from every veil of duality and all problems. We just *are* the Self, a simple being without problems. Filled by this unbounded being, we are free to accept life as it is and to live in a state of deep well-being, peace, and gratitude, regardless of external circumstances.

We recognize and experience the fundamental core of existence not as frightening emptiness but as uplifting fullness. We enter a state of pure awareness that makes it possible to take in and appreciate all that is living and potentially alive. This awareness carries us beyond all polarization, beyond profit and loss, victory and defeat, temporary happiness and sadness. We go through life with full attention to the fundamental essence that gave rise to us, and that we still and forever are. Our existence is filled with *satchitananda*: being, consciousness, bliss. This is a natural state available to anyone willing and able to open up and surrender.

To the extent that we can see our life patterns as expressions of the cosmic play of the Self, our karma dissolves. It simply has no power to capture our attention in the same way anymore. Instead of getting stuck in the "problems" we before had a habit of seeing, we instead see all that happens as a natural unfolding of Consciousness. If we manage to hold on to that wide-open viewpoint, we have attained what is called in the texts of Kashmir Shaivism *jivan mukti*, the state of freedom while alive. The Self is finally enough unto itself, and we enjoy this reality every second. We experience everything as the symphony of the Self. We appreciate and digest all that we meet on our life's path as spiritual nourishment.

To approach and achieve this state, we need neither repress nor deny our karma. Rather, we rise above it in surrender and recognition. Then karma loses its power over us. Its web is powerless to ensnare us. We are liberated. From a non-dualistic perspective, the web shines on us as manifest Consciousness.

NOTES

1. Rudi (Albert Rudolph, later Swami Rudrananda) was born in Brooklyn, New York, in 1928 and grew up under very difficult circumstances. From an early age, he was conscious of his spiritual potential, and he talked about having had visions and experiences with Tibetan teachers as a child. In his early adult years, he worked actively with his spiritual development, most importantly as a student of Shri Shankaracharya of Puri. During the 1950s, Rudi opened an oriental antiques store in the Greenwich Village neighborhood of New York City. Within a few years, the store became one of the finest of its kind in United States. In 1958, while traveling in India, Rudi was taken by an acquaintance to an ashram in Ganeshpuri outside Mumbai to meet the person who was to become his root guru, Bhagavan Nityananda. The meeting was of such depth that it totally changed the direction of Rudi's life. By the later years of his life, Rudi had become a truly extraordinary being and teacher. He trained hundreds of students and had a profound influence on all who came in contact with him, both in the United States and overseas. He departed this world in a plane crash in 1973. The basis for Rudi's teaching was his deep personal wish to grow.

2. The karma theory is described in very early Indian philosophical texts. The most well-known text that addresses the effects of karma and how to be free from the wheel of karma is the Bhagavad Gita, which is discussed in Chapter 7.

3. Swami Rudrananda (Rudi) introduced the concepts horizontal and vertical in his book *Spiritual Cannibalism*. New York: Links Books, 1973. http://www.internetyoga.com/spiritCannibal/index.htm

4. Laszlo, Ervin (in Norwegian, published in English with the title *Science and The Akasha Field*) *Revolusjon i vitenskapen, fremveksten av det holistiske paradigm*. Oslo: Flux forlag, 2003.

5 Talks with Sri Nisargadatta Maharaj, AbeBooks.com: I Am That, Chetana (P) Ltd., Mumbai, India, 1973

6. Bhagavan Nityananda, Sutra 65, *The Sky of the Heart: Jewels of Wisdom from Nityananda.* Portland, Ore.: Rudra Press, 1996. Nityananda was my teacher Rudi's root guru.

7. The double breath exercise was given by Swami Rudrananda (Rudi) to his meditation students.

8. The tantric text Vijnana Bhairava (Divine Consciousness). The text is a chapter from the *Rudrayamala Tantra*, a <u>Bhairava</u> <u>Agama</u>. <u>Devi</u>, the goddess, asks Shiva to reveal the essence of the way to realization of the highest reality. In his answer Shiva describes 112 ways to enter into the universal and transcendental state of consciousness. References to it appear throughout the literature of Kashmir Shaivism, indicating that it was considered to be an important text in the monistic school of Kashmir Shaiva philosophy.

9. Laszlo, Ervin (in Norwegian, published in English with the title *The Akasha Field) Revolusjon i vitenskapen, fremveksten av det holistiske paradigmet.* Flux forlag, Oslo, Norway, 2003, p. 9.

10. Pratyabhijnarhdayam: The Secret of Self-Recognition. Delhi, India: Motil Banarsidass, 1980.

11. Mascaro, Juan (translator). *Bhagavad Gita.* New York: Penguin Books, 1962, pp. 48-49.

12. In later texts, Vishnu is called Shiva.

13. Mascaro, Juan (translator). *Bhagavad Gita.* New York: Penguin Books, 1962,, p. 49.

14. Ibid p. 121.

15. Ibid p. 122.

16. Jens Braarvik, in the introduction to his Norwegian translation of *The*

Bhagavad Gita.

17. Cited from memory by the author, who was present when it was said by Swami Rudrananda (Rudi).

18. Lao-tzu. *Tao te Ching.* New York: Vintage Books, a Division of Random House, 1972, verse 81

19. Mahatma Gandhi, *The Story of My Experiments With Truth*, BN Publishing 2008

20. Helminski, Edmund, *The Ruins of the of the Heart, Selected Poems by Jelaluddin Rumi.* Putney, Vt.: Threshold Books, 1981.

21. Lampl, M. and Johnson, M. L. "Identifying Saltatory Growth Patterns in Infancy: A Comparison of Results Based on Measurement Protocol. " *American Journal of Human Biology* 9 (3), (1997), pp. 343-355.

22. Ibsen, Henrik. *Peer Gynt* (in Norwegian). Oslo: Gyldendal klassiker, Gyldendal forlag, 2005.

ABOUT THE AUTHOR

Acharya Premananda (born Per Oskar Johansen) has many years experience as a practitioner of meditation before becoming a spiritual mentor and meditation master. Today he serves many people in this capacity.

For more than 45 years, he has practiced, a simple and effective approach to inner work based on what he learned from his root guru Swami Rudrananda (Rudi) in New York in the 1970's. Premananda now lives in Europe and holds regular retreats and programs in various locations.

Premananda was a student of Swami Rudrananda in New York City from the fall of 1969 until Rudi's passing in 1973. He counts his lineage back to Bhagavan Nityananda who was Rudi's guru. After Rudi's passing, Premananda was for many years connected with and continued to practice and develop in an ashram established by Rudi in the US. He has also studied Kashmir Shaivism and other Indian traditions, as well as Tibetan Buddhist practices.

Premananda has written books and articles about spiritual practice, most notably "Open Your Eyes Within". He has a doctorate degree in education and was for five years professor at the University of Tennessee, Knoxville, USA. While serving as a professor, he also taught meditation and ran a local meditation center. Since 1983, he worked for many years as a consultant and trainer in industry, with a focus on improvement methods and team work. While doing this, he regularly taught meditation and served as a spiritual mentor.

CPSIA information can be obtained
at www.ICGtesting.com
Printed in the USA
LVHW05s1446041010
592411LV00009B/655/P

9 781722 182342